Saving the Ants

and 58 other Kids Sermons from the Gospel of Matthew

Ruth Gilmore

Augsburg

MINNEAPOLIS

*To the good folks
at the Lutheran Church
of the Good Shepherd, Sacramento;
thank you for your enthusiasm,
encouragement, and love.*

SAVING THE ANTS
and 58 Other Kids Sermons from the Gospel of Matthew

Large-quantity purchases or custom editions of this book are available at a discount from the publisher. For more information, contact the sales department at Augsburg Fortress, Publishers, 1-800-328-4648, or write to: Sales Director, Augsburg Fortress, Publishers, P.O. Box 1209, Minneapolis, MN 55440-1209.

Scripture passages marked NIV are from the Holy Bible, New International Version, copyright © 1973, 1978, 1984 International Bible Society. Used by permission of Zondervan Publishing House. All rights reserved.

Scripture quotations marked NLT are taken from the Holy Bible, New Living Translation, copyright © 1996. Used by permission of Tyndale House Publishers, Inc., Wheaton, Illinois 60189. All rights reserved.

Scripture passages marked NRSV are from the New Revised Standard Version of the Bible, copyright © 1946, 1952, 1971, 1989 by the Division of Christian Education of the National Council of the Churches of Christ in the USA. Used by permission.

Scripture passages marked RSV are from the Revised Standard Version of the Bible, copyright © 1946, 1952, 1971, 1989 by the Division of Christian Education of the National Council of the Churches of Christ in the USA. Used by permission.

Cover design by Marti Naughton; cover graphics by EyeWire
Book design by Michelle L. N. Cook

Library of Congress Cataloging-in-Publication Data
Gilmore, Ruth, 1962–
    Saving the ants : and 58 other kids sermons from the Gospel of Matthew / by Ruth Gilmore.
       p.cm.
    ISBN 0-8066-4080-4 (alk. paper)
    1. Children's sermons. 2. Church year sermons. 3. Bible. N.T. Matthew—Sermons. 4. Sermons, American—21st century. 5. Lutheran Church–Sermons. I. Title.
BV4315.G388 2001
252'.53—dc21   2001041240

The paper used in this publication meets the minimum requirements of American National Standard for Information Sciences—Permanence of Paper for Printed Library Materials, ANSI Z329.48-1984. ♾ ™

Manufactured in the U.S.A.   AF 9-4080

05   04   03   02   2   3   4   5   6   7   8   9   10

Contents

Foreword
by Walter Wangerin, Jr.

Ruth Gilmore has gathered together bright, brief patterns for communicating core truths of lessons in the Revised Common Lectionary.

As worship itself engages more than half our senses, so sound, sight, touch, motion, and discovery—and the near presence of the storyteller—all draw children, Sunday by Sunday, chapter by chapter, into the one real story of our salvation.

Here are little stories. Here are suggestions for tactile interaction. Here are frameworks for your own personal stories.

But the proclamation itself waits for you and for the dramatic moment when you engage the senses, the fierce interest, and the hearts of children.

Two things only will fill Gilmore's bright patterns with the power of a living Lord, and both things are called by the same name: love.

If you love the Lord of the story with your entire being, your telling will find its most persuasive style, *your* style, the manner you use when there is nothing more important to tell another soul than this. In you, the story will flare and live—and you, your presence, and your person, will become the manifest evidence of it.

And if you love the children arrayed before you, you will design and tell that story specifically for *them*. You will watch them and be alert to their tiniest signs of attention. You will rejoice when the story goes home to their hearts, and they will see your joy, and their delight will grow even keener.

As Ruth Gilmore invites you to proclamation in these pieces, accept the invitation with love!

Introduction

"Let the little children come to me, and do not hinder them, for the kingdom of heaven belongs to such as these" (Matt. 19:14 NIV). Jesus' words remind us to see a child through the eyes of God—not as a noisy distraction from business at hand but as an honored inheritor of God's kingdom and a model of humility. Children, dancing their way through life, not yet filled with pride and self, still delightfully saturated with the joy of living—*they* embrace the kingdom. They live in the moment of grace.

This book offers fifty-nine chances to interact with children during worship services. Children's time is a magical moment in the church service. When young ones are invited forward, many will spring from their seats and gallop to the front of the church, thrilled to sit next to you and have the attention of the whole congregation. And the idea of hearing a good story told just for them or the chance to unravel the meaning of an intriguing object lesson—well, these are opportunities just too good to pass up.

So, right from the start, all the advantages belong to you.

Stories have power.

Even as you capture the children's attention, adults in the congregation will be drawn into the story, hearing Bible truths told in a new way, appreciating the simplicity you bring to the message. We are—all of us—children, the sons and daughters of our heavenly Parent. Jesus reaches out to the child in each of us, teaching through stories and parables, because all children love a good story.

The sermons in this book ask you to be a storyteller. Each one is self-contained and ready to use. But before you begin, here are tips to sharpen your storytelling skills and make these children's sermons the most effective they can be.

Use sermons that work for you.

If you are following the Revised Common Lectionary, you will find that each sermon is based on one of the texts for the day. There are fifty-nine sermons in all, covering the entire church year, including special non-Sunday events and festivals. If you are not following a lectionary, you can search the contents list by theme to find applicable sermons.

Build relationships.

Many sermons in this book make use of a personal anecdote or illustration. Children love to hear real-life stories about their elders, especially if they like the elders who are telling the stories. The relationship with your listeners has a lot to do with the connection you build in your first moments with them. It is important to be on their level—physically as well as intellectually. Sit with the children and recognize the importance of each child with your gestures and eye contact. Make it clear that you are eager to travel into the story with them.

And it's good to remember that our preconceived ideas about teaching and learning may be wrong. Even though we might really want our listeners to sit quietly and keep their eyes glued on us, some children learn best while in motion. Some of my most active listeners often turn out to be ones who most fully understand the point I am trying to make.

Keep it simple, brief, concrete.

I have tried to keep the language of these sermons simple, direct, and easily understandable to children. Most sermons will take five minutes or less to deliver. Children's attention is a tenuous and precious thing. They are intent on soaking in every miracle of the world around them, and to concentrate on one thing at a time is a considerable challenge.

Many sermons make use of a simple object to illustrate a lesson. (A brief note at the beginning of some sermons will alert you to any special preparations or props.) Children will understand and retain more as more of their five senses are engaged. Their sense of touch or smell or taste will draw them back into the sermon and remind them of the truth that was taught. And with God's grace, they will learn that truth by heart.

Make the sermons your own—the CD-ROM.

As was noted earlier, these sermons can be used just as they are—read directly from the page. *But they will be even better with a bit of preparation and personalization.* Use the enclosed CD to customize each sermon for the most appropriate delivery for your situation, for your audience. Add or substitute your own interesting, relevant stories wherever possible. Build in anecdotes, illustrations, and names from your congregation, city, or community.

Prepare.

It's always better to tell your sermon than to read it. The more familiar you are with the sermon, the easier it will be to *talk* to your listeners. In a well-rehearsed play, the trappings of the performance fade into the background while the emotion and meaning of the play come into focus. A performer who knows a part well is able to ad-lib if the occasion demands.

And while you are sharing your sermons, don't be surprised if a kid puts his or her oar in. That may shift your direction slightly; but if you're prepared, you can go with the flow while continuing to steer gently. The bank you end up traveling to may be more interesting and important than the place you were originally headed.

Visit our Web site, too!

If you have a Web browser, helpful information and resources about children's sermons are available at <**www.kidsermons.com**>. There you'll be able to contact the author, read anecdotes, download scripts for puppet shows,

Saving the Ants

find information about other books in the series, and access links to other helpful sites on the Internet. The Web site has an online index of all currently available kids sermons by Ruth Gilmore. They are listed by biblical reference in order from the Old Testament to the New Testament.

Finally, enjoy the rewards.
God has generously blessed me through the children who have sat with me on the steps of the altar. I marvel to see how young children can catch the meaning behind stories before I've even gotten to the explanations. I rejoice in the delightful insights of my young audiences. I suspect that, through the years, they have taught me far more than I have taught them.

May God bless you as you teach the children—and, in teaching them, welcome the Lord Jesus himself into your midst.

Surprise Inspection

Today is a very special day, isn't it? It's the first Sunday in the season of Advent. We'll spend the next four weeks getting ready to welcome the Christ Child at Christmas. We get the church ready by putting up new cloths on the altar, and bringing out the Advent wreath and lighting the first candle. *(You may describe the Advent preparations at your own church.)* We may get our own homes ready for Christmas by cleaning and decorating. Do any of you put decorations up for Christmas? *(Let children discuss their preparations.)*

Are any of you going to have company at your home during Christmas vacation? *(Children can share their plans.)* If a guest is coming to visit, we usually try to get the house ready. We clean and put things away and prepare a room for the guest. How many of you have to clean your rooms or pick up your toys? I know I have to clean up my room and pick up my toys when someone special is coming over.

Let's play a little game this morning. It's called "Surprise Inspection." You pretend that you're cleaning your room, and I'll pretend that I'm coming to check your work to see that you're all done. I won't warn you that I'm coming, I'll just say "Inspection!" You have to be done cleaning when I say "Inspection!" Now here's the hard part. I want you to raise your hands up over your head just before I say "Inspection!" to show me that you really are ready. Okay, everyone close their eyes and get your hands busy like you're cleaning your room.

(Wait a few moments and encourage all hands to be busy, and all eyes to be closed, then surprise them by quickly saying

"Inspection!" Most of the hands will still be moving.) Inspection! All hands up in the air. You can open your eyes now. Did any of you put your hands up in the air before I said "Inspection"? It's hard to know exactly when the inspection is coming, isn't it? Sometimes we might be told to have our room clean by the time they check on us again, and we're not always ready when they come back.

During Advent, we're getting ready to receive a very special guest. Jesus is coming! We prepare our churches and homes, but we also prepare our hearts to welcome Jesus. We don't want to get so busy during Advent that we forget to pray to God or think about the birth of Jesus. It's fun to put up decorations and make cards and presents for other people. We just have to remember, though, that we're really preparing to welcome Jesus. We want to be ready to welcome him at Christmas and when he comes down to earth once more.

Dear Jesus, help us to prepare our hearts and lives to welcome you this Advent. Keep us from becoming too busy to remember why we celebrate Christmas.

Notes

Making a Path

Preparation: Bring several tools for clearing brush or raking that one might use for making a path through a patch of brambles. If tools aren't available, you may use pictures to illustrate.

I want you to imagine that you live in a little cottage in the forest. You have lived there by yourself for quite a while and you haven't had any visitors, so the pathway to the house has become overgrown with vines and brambles. One day, Jesus comes to visit, but he can't reach your door. He stands at the edge of the thicket and calls to you, "Clear the pathway! I want to come to your house!"

What might you do to get the path cleared so that Jesus could reach your house? What tools could you use? *(Discuss the possibilities with the children. Some examples follow.)* You could use a branch cutter on the thick vines and brambles. A shovel would be useful for digging out roots or removing big rocks. You could rake the path clear of old leaves and sticks or use a broom to sweep away dirt and sand. *(You may show some examples of tools to children or pass around some of the smaller, safer tools, such as a trowel or short broom and dustpan.)*

Do you think it would be hard work clearing a path through a bunch of thorns and brambles? If the path were really overgrown it might take all day. But knowing that Jesus was waiting to visit us would help us work harder and get the job done so that his path was clear.

The Bible describes someone who made a path for Jesus. "He is a voice shouting in the wilderness: 'Prepare a pathway for the Lord's coming! Make a straight road for him!'" (Matt. 3:3 NLT). This was John the Baptist, getting the people ready to hear the message that Jesus was bringing. John didn't use shovels or rakes to get the path ready for Jesus; he used his words.

The brambles and thorns that John wanted people to clear out of their lives were the bad habits and thoughts that kept people far away from God. John told people to repent, to stop doing the things that made God sad and to start living lives that made God happy. John told people to clear their hearts and minds so that they would be ready to welcome Jesus when he came.

This is the second week of Advent, and Christmas is coming closer. We need to remember to keep the path to our hearts clear so that Jesus can come to us this Christmas. We can keep the path clear by praying and reading the Bible and remembering that Christmas isn't about getting things; it's about Jesus being born.

Forgive us, Lord, for letting the thorns and brambles grow in our lives. Clear a path to our hearts, Lord Jesus. We want you to come in.

Notes

Should We Keep Looking?

One more Sunday and Christmas will almost be here. Have you been keeping the path to your heart open for Jesus to come in? During this time of the year, when it seems like everyone is searching for just the right gifts for their family and friends, we need to remember to look for Jesus, the Savior, and make room in our hearts for him.

The Gospel lesson for today talks about the disciples of John the Baptist. They asked Jesus, "Are you really the Messiah we've been waiting for? Or should we keep looking for someone else?" Jesus replied, "Go back to John and tell him about what you have heard and seen—the blind see . . . the deaf hear, the dead are raised to life, and the Good News is being preached to the poor" (Matt. 11:3-5 NLT).

John and his disciples had been waiting and looking for the Messiah for so long, they wanted to be sure Jesus was the one. Jesus had to remind them of all the miracles and wonderful things that had been happening since he began preaching. So many things pointed to the truth that Jesus was the true Messiah. The Savior of the world was here.

This search for the Messiah is like waiting for Christmas Day to arrive. We know that Christmas is coming. The signs are everywhere. Lights glow on houses and stores, green trees are decorated with beautiful ornaments, presents are appearing under the trees, and packages arrive in the mail. Christmas is coming, but it seems like such a long time to wait until it's finally here!

To the disciples, it seemed as if they had been waiting forever for God's Promised One, the Messiah, to arrive.

When Jesus finally came, did they need to keep looking? No. The Savior sent by God was finally around them. It would have been foolish to keep looking. When Christmas morning finally arrives, do we have to keep waiting and counting the days until it's here? No. When Christmas comes, we can celebrate! We don't have to keep waiting.

As we wait for Christmas to come, we know that we have found the one that the world has been waiting for. Jesus is the Messiah, the Savior of our world. We don't have to keep looking. We have found God's son, Jesus. And that is why we celebrate Christmas.

Father in heaven, thank you for sending your son, Jesus, to the world. We're glad that we don't have to keep looking and searching. We have found the Messiah.

Notes

God with Us

When you were born, you were each given something that is very important to you. It is something that you use now; and you will use it the rest of your life. The thing that you were given at birth is something that you share with others. In fact, if you never share this gift with anyone, then it cannot be used. Can you guess what this gift is? *(Let children discuss possible answers; you may guide them.)* When you were born, each of you was given a name. Can you tell me what some of your names are? *(Children may share their names.)* Do any of you have other names, such as nicknames or middle names? *(Discuss.)*

Jesus was given his name before he was born. He was God's son and many months before he was born, God told Joseph and Mary to name him "Jesus." The name *Jesus* means "the Lord saves." This name was important because Jesus was sent by God to save the world from sin. Do any of you know what your names mean? *(Discuss with children; you may offer the meaning of your own name as well.)*

Jesus had other names, too. He was also called "Immanuel," which means "God with us." Jesus was God's son, but he was also God himself, appearing here on earth to be with the people of the world. Jesus is given many other names in the Bible, and all of them tell us something about who Jesus is and what he does for us.

In the Old Testament book of Isaiah, Jesus is called "Wonderful Counselor." That would mean someone who was wise and could give good advice and comfort; someone who we can go to with all of our problems. He is also called

"Mighty God." That means that he is powerful and rules over everything. "Everlasting Father" is another name for Jesus. This shows us that the Father and the Son are one, and that Jesus is eternal; he will never die. Jesus is also called the "Prince of Peace," meaning that he is the ruler, but he does not rule by force. Jesus does not bring wars or fighting; Jesus brings peace.

All of these names tell us about Jesus. But during Advent and Christmas, the name of Jesus that we think about the most is the name "Immanuel." During Advent, we sing the hymn "Oh Come, Oh Come, Immanuel." Jesus is God with us. The baby born at Christmas was God himself coming to live with us here on earth. "Immanuel" may sound like a strange name; it's not a very common name, but it reminds us of something very important. When we invite Jesus in our hearts, God is right here with us.

Our Lord Jesus, Immanuel, come and live in our hearts. Thank you for being with us and coming to our world at Christmas.

Notes

Saving the Ants

Preparation: Bring a toy ant or a picture and, if possible, a jar of real ants.

Tonight is very special, isn't it? It's Christmas Eve, the night of Jesus' birth! Can you imagine being at the manger the night when Jesus was born? Mary and Joseph would be there, watching their newborn son all wrapped up, so tiny and so amazing. They knew that night in the stable that the Almighty God himself had come to earth as a helpless human baby. God had sent his Son to the world to save all people.

There were other creatures there at the manger, too, besides humans. What other animals do you suppose saw the baby Jesus? *(Let children name some of the animals.)* Do you suppose there were any very tiny creatures that looked something like this? *(Show toy ant.)* There are ants all over the world, aren't there? I'm sure there were some ants near the stable. And real ants aren't usually big like this toy ant; they are extremely tiny. Real ants are this small. *(Show jar of ants.)*

Let's say that you really loved ants. Let's say that there was an ant colony near your house. You were careful not to step on those ants, and you would even leave food out for them. Let's say that you loved each individual ant and wished that they could know that you loved them.

How in the world could you talk to an ant? *(Let children offer their ideas.)* Even if you got down on your belly and tried to look a teeny ant in the eye, you couldn't make the ant understand. The only way that you're going to get through to those ants is to become an ant yourself. Can you imagine being an ant? Especially a very tiny one? It would be a dangerous experiment. You could get squashed. Maybe you would go through all that trouble to become an ant and they wouldn't even listen to you. The ants that you love might drive you away. You might try to warn them about a flood or a fire that was coming and explain to them that you became an ant so that you could save them. Some might listen to you and others might not. But becoming an ant would be the only way to really communicate.

Well, what did God do? The Infinite Creator, the Almighty God, loved the people of the world so much, that he made himself as tiny as a baby, so that he could talk to us. And God told us through Jesus that he loves us more than anything. God came to earth at Christmas, and that is why we celebrate. Merry Christmas, everyone! *(Hold up your ants and greet them as well.)* Merry Christmas, little ants.

Dear Lord, thank you for sending your son, Jesus, to our earth to show us how much you love us.

Notes

Unwrapping the Gift

Preparation: Find five boxes, each one fitting inside the other. Wrap each box separately, placing a small envelope inside each box that you wrap. The envelope can contain, for example, stickers, candies, or bookmarks. The last box should contain small crosses to hand out.

Merry Christmas, everyone! Today we celebrate the wonderful gift that God gave to the world. God sent his only son, Jesus, to us to bring us life and salvation. God gave us the gift of Jesus. We give each other gifts at Christmas, too. So I thought it would be fun to bring a gift to unwrap and share.

This is not a normal gift. You will soon see that this box is a little bit like the gift of Jesus. When Jesus arrived on earth, what did people see? Did Jesus look like an important person? Jesus was wrapped in swaddling clothes sort of like a present is wrapped up. When his mother, Mary, unwrapped those clothes to change him, there was just a baby inside. But there was more to Jesus than just what people saw at first.

Let's unwrap this box and see if there's more to this present than what we see on the outside. *(Open box, find envelope, and have a helper hand out small gifts while you continue to talk.)* There is a gift inside this box, but it also contains another box that needs to be unwrapped.

As Jesus grew, people soon realized there was much more to Jesus. There were many gifts in this person. Jesus taught in the temple when he was only twelve, amazing the grownups with his wisdom. *(Open next box and hand out gifts.)*

Then Jesus began his ministry, and people saw that he had the gift of healing. He could make blind people see and lame people walk. With his miracles, Jesus brought joy to people wherever he went. *(Open next box and hand out gifts.)*

The crowds followed Jesus, and he preached to them and taught them about God's love. Their lives were changed as they learned that God loved them and cared about them. *(Open next box and hand out gifts.)* So many gifts in one person.

Finally, Jesus was led to the cross to do what he came to do. He died on the cross to take away our sin and rose again on Easter morning to beat death forever. *(Open last box, which should contain an envelope with smaller crosses to hand out.)* This last gift is one that lasts forever. When we go to heaven we will spend forever with God and all of the believers.

The gift of Jesus at Christmas was much greater than anyone at that time knew. It was the best gift the world has ever been given.

We praise you, Lord, for the priceless gift of your son, Jesus. Thank you for sending your son to our world. Thank you for the best gift of all.

Notes

Good Creativity

Preparation: Bring sheets of paper and pencils to hand out.

It's the first Sunday after Christmas, and we're starting a new church year. We're at the beginning again. If we look at the beginning of the Bible in the book of Genesis, what are the first words we read? Does anyone remember how the Bible begins? *(Let children respond.)* It reads, "In the beginning God created the heavens and the earth" (Gen. 1:1 NLT). God saw that it was good. God created good things, and God is a wonderfully creative God.

In the beginning, God created something in his own image. Do you know what that was? *(Children may offer answers.)* It was humans. People are a special creation made by God. So if our God is creative and he made us to be like him, do you think people were made to be creative? Yes! We can create pictures and music. We can invent dances and stories.

We're all creative in different ways. Some people are really good artists. They can draw pictures that look like the real thing and that are beautiful. I'm not very good at drawing, but I tried to draw a picture of a person. I'll show it to you. *(You may or may not have a talent for drawing, but make a picture anyway and show your sketch to children.)* I've seen lots of pictures drawn by different artists of many different things, and I've realized that we can be creative for good and, sadly enough, we can be creative for bad.

(Here you may offer your own story of creativity being used in a bad way. An example follows.) When I was little, I remember

my brothers and sisters and I would sometimes tease each other and try to make each other mad by drawing pictures. We would scribble a really ugly picture on a piece of paper, something like this *(show second picture)*, and we would say to each other, "This is what you look like!" And they would draw an even uglier picture and say, "Well, this is what you look like!" That was being creative in a bad way, trying to hurt each other's feelings with the things we created.

I drew another picture here, and this picture tries to show how my family makes me feel and how I feel about them. *(Show picture and talk about it.)* I can use these pens and paper to make bad things or good things. In the same way, each one of us can use our lives to make good or bad things.

Before you go back to your seats, I'd like for everyone to take a piece of blank paper and draw or write some of the good things you plan to do in the coming new year. May God bless your good creations.

Thank you, Creator God, for blessing us with creative talents. Help us to make good things with our creativity.

Notes

Recognition

Preparation (Optional): Bring a puppet or stuffed animal duckling as a prop.

D o you know who I am? Do you recognize me? *(Let children respond.)* Can you recognize your family? Do you remember the first time that you looked into your mom's face and knew who that person was? That was a long time ago. Tiny little babies only a few months old can recognize the face of their mommy or daddy. They look at that familiar, loving face and they smile and reach out for a hug. It's amazing how soon babies will recognize the people who love them and who helped to create them. It would, in fact, be strange if they didn't recognize them.

Even baby birds can usually recognize their moms once they learn what they look and sound like. *(Duckling prop can be used here.)* When ducklings hatch, they immediately look around for something to follow. Of course, the first thing they see is usually their mother. They follow their mother, and she teaches them all the things they need to know to become grown-up ducks. Sometimes it happens that a nest of baby ducks hatch out while the mama bird is not around. Then, if a dog comes trotting by, those little ducks follow the dog.

This doesn't work out so well, though. A dog wouldn't make a very good mama duck. He couldn't teach the ducklings how to find the kind of food that ducks eat. He couldn't teach the ducklings how to fly or where to fly in the winter. If the real mama duck showed up later, the poor ducklings might not recognize her.

It is very important to know who you belong to. It is very important to know who made you. Can anyone tell me who created the world? *(Children may answer.)* God created the world. In the Gospel of John, we learn that in the beginning Jesus was with God and everything was created with love, through Jesus.

Did everyone recognize Jesus when he came to earth? Did everyone know that he came to save them and did everyone believe in him? Not everyone did. Even now, some people are like those poor little ducklings following the wrong mama. I'm very glad that each one of you can recognize your mom and dad. And I'm especially glad that all of you know your loving God. I hope and pray that you will continue to follow Jesus. He has a lot to teach you.

Father in heaven, thank you for creating us. We want to follow you and learn from you always.

Notes

Healing Spirit

How many of you were baptized when you were little? *(Children can raise their hands.)* That was an important day, wasn't it? On the day that you were baptized, you were welcomed into the family of God, and Jesus came to live in your heart. Did you know that Jesus was baptized, too? Today we celebrate the baptism of our Lord.

Does anyone know where Jesus was baptized? *(Children may respond.)* Jesus was baptized in the Jordan River. That was an important day for Jesus. Right after Jesus was baptized, he came up out of the water and the sky opened up and the Spirit of God came down to him like a beautiful dove. And from the time of his baptism on, Jesus was filled with God's powerful spirit, and he did amazing things.

When Jesus began to preach about God, he healed many, many people. We have doctors nowadays who can heal people with medicine, but Jesus could heal people simply by touching them. We may have been baptized and so we have God's spirit, but can we heal people just by touching them? *(Children may respond.)* Not usually. God still does miracles today through ordinary people, but Jesus was very special, wasn't he? He was the Son of God, and he could heal anything.

Do you think that you have any healing power in your hands? This may surprise you, but you do have healing power. The God of love is in your heart and your hands can help someone whose feelings have been hurt. Have you ever seen someone who is crying or feeling bad? *(Let children answer.)* You might have gone over to that person and put your hand on their shoulder or you might have given them a big hug, and made them feel better, just by touching them. If you did, then you have been a healer.

If you fall down and scrape your knee, you can put a bandage on your cut to help it heal. But sometimes we hurt inside. Sometimes kids are sad; even mommies and daddies can be sad. *(Here you may give your own example of being comforted. An example follows.)* If I'm feeling bad and one of my children wraps his or her arms around me and gives me a big hug, it always makes me feel better. Little hands are great for healing.

God's spirit of love and healing is inside each one of you. Remember that God can use your hands to heal and to make people feel better.

Give each of us a spirit of healing, Lord. Help us to be your comforting and healing hands in our world today.

Notes

Comfort to Comfort

Preparation: Bring a big blanket or quilt.

Raise your hand if you've ever felt really cold. Most of us know what it's like to shiver in cold weather. Let's pretend that it's really cold in here this morning. I brought a blanket along just in case I get too cold. Right now, I'm feeling warm enough myself, but let's say that I notice the person sitting next to me is shivering. *(Indicate a child sitting near you.)* I may be feeling warm, but I remember how I feel when I'm cold. I know that when I'm cold I really appreciate a warm blanket. So what do you think I should do? *(Let children respond.)* I can share my blanket with that person, and warm them up.

What if I had never been cold in my life? Would I know how that person who was shivering from the cold felt? I wouldn't know, and maybe I wouldn't know how to help. Jesus came to earth as a human and lived with us. He felt cold like us. He felt loneliness like we sometimes do. God knows how we feel.

In Second Corinthians, chapter 1, Paul writes, "[God] comforts us in all our troubles so that we can comfort others. When others are troubled, we will be able to give them the same comfort God has given us" (v. 4 NLT).

God comforts us so that we can comfort others. How many of you have ever felt lonely in your life? If you have felt lonely, you know how great it feels to have someone talk to you and ask to be your friend. So then when you see someone else who looks lonely or left out, you know that you can help by talking to him or her and being a friend.

Our Heavenly Father gives us comfort, and we pass it on to others, and they pass it on, too. I'd like to see how quickly you all can pass my comfort quilt around so that everyone has a chance to touch it and hand it on to someone else. When you hand it to the next person, say "Comfort" as you pass it. *(Pass quilt or blanket around so that it comes back to you.)*

I'd like for someone who is good at comforting others to do something for me. Raise your hand if you are a good comforter. *(Choose a volunteer and hand them your blanket.)* On your way back to your seat, I'd like you to find someone in the congregation who looks like they could use a soft blanket and give this blanket to them. They can use it until the end of the service and give it back to me later. Thank you for remembering to pass comfort on to others.

Dear Lord, thank you for being our comforter. As you comfort and help us, show us how we can comfort and help others.

Notes

A Great Light

Preparation: Bring a big blanket and a flashlight.

How many of you have ever tried to walk in the dark? Have you ever gotten up in the middle of the night and tried to walk to the bathroom, for example? Maybe you forgot to pick up some sharp little toy and you stepped on it in the dark. It can be very difficult and even painful to walk around when it's really dark.

(You can share a story about your experience trying to walk in darkness. An example follows.) Sometimes, when I walk out the front door in the dark, I hear a crunch, which means that I have just stepped on a snail that has crept out to eat some tender flowers at night. Or if I'm walking through the house in my bare feet with no lights on, sometimes I'll stub my toe on a chair leg. Walking in the dark can be dangerous.

If everyone scoots in real close, we'll see how many people we can get under this dark blanket. *(Gather with the children under the blanket.)* It's pretty dark under here, isn't it? I wanted to read a Bible verse to you, but now it's so dark I don't know if I can. But I think I have something that might help. *(Retrieve the flashlight out of your bag.)* This flashlight will really help; just the thing to push back the darkness. *(Turn on the light.)* That makes a big difference, doesn't it? I can see much better. Here's the Bible verse; Isaiah, chapter 9, "The people who walked in darkness have seen a great light; those who lived in a land of deep darkness—on them light has shined" (v. 2 NRSV).

Let's push back the darkness and take the blanket off now. *(Remove blanket.)* Can anyone answer this question; who is the "light of the world"? Someone said, "I am the light of the world." Who was that? *(Let children answer.)* That was Jesus!

Jesus is the light that came into our dark world. Jesus shows us where bad things are so we can avoid them. We don't have to bump into the bad things because Jesus shines brightly and shows us the right way to go. The people who walked in the darkness, bumping into things, have seen a great light! Jesus Christ is the Light of the world.

Thanks for coming up this morning. Be careful as you go back to your seats, though, and try not to bump into anything on the way.

Jesus, you are the Light of the world! Thank you for shining in our lives to show us the way we should go.

Notes

Blessed Are . . .

Preparation: Bring a ball or inflatable globe and a whistle.

How many of you play ball games at school? Would you like to play now? *(Choose a few volunteers to play.)* The object of the game is to get the ball for yourself. Don't play too rough; treat each other gently. When you hear me blow the whistle, you have to freeze. *(Begin game; blow whistle before it becomes too rough.)* Okay, would you like to know who won? *(Take the ball and give it to a child who has been quietly watching the fray.)* This meek one sitting here quietly gets the ball. That's a strange sort of game, isn't it?

This is a little bit like what Jesus talked about in the "Sermon on the Mount." Jesus said, "God blesses those who realize their need for him, for the Kingdom of Heaven is given to them. . . . God blesses those who are gentle and lowly, for the whole earth will belong to them. . . . God blesses those who are merciful, for they will be shown mercy" (Matt. 5: 3, 5, 7 NLT).

The world says just the opposite. Here are some things you might hear on television or at school. You may even hear this kind of talk from other kids or even from some grownups: "It's better to be rich and proud, so that you can take whatever you want. It's better to be bold and pushy; that way you can conquer the earth. If you want to win, you can't worry about hurting other people."

Those aren't the sorts of things that Jesus taught, are they?

This ball is sort of like the earth and as far back as we know, there have been people fighting over the earth. Now, it may look like they own the earth for a while, but in reality the creator who made the earth is in control. And Jesus says that the meek ones who look to God will inherit the earth.

Now, this doesn't mean that you shouldn't ever win at ball games or shouldn't try your best. It does mean that we should put God first in our lives and think of others before ourselves. It means that we should remember how much we need God in our lives. The more we understand and live the words of Jesus, the more we know that the truth is just the opposite of what the world says. The truth is in the words of Jesus, "God blesses those who are gentle and lowly, for the whole earth will belong to them" (Matt. 5:5 NLT).

Dear Lord of heaven and earth, help us to remember not to grab things for ourselves. Help us to wait for the gifts that you give.

Notes

Salt and Light

Preparation: Bring salt and flour, or do your taste test with salted and unsalted chips.

Jesus once told his disciples that they were salt and light. That was sort of a strange thing to say. What do you suppose Jesus meant by that? Jesus told his disciples, "You are the salt of the earth. But what good is salt if it has lost its flavor? Can you make it useful again? It will be thrown out and trampled underfoot as useless" (Matt 5:13 NLT). In other words, without its strong taste, salt is not much good for anything.

Could I have a volunteer to taste something for me? *(Choose a child to try a flour and salt taste test.)* I'm going to pour a white powder into your hand. You taste it and tell me if you think it is salt or not. *(Put a pinch of white flour into the child's hand.)* Does that taste like salt? *(Child can describe the taste.)* It doesn't have much of a taste, does it? It's bland and plain. Would you put it on your food?

Now I want you to taste something else. *(Put a pinch of salt into child's hand; it can be ground to a powder to resemble flour.)* Does that have a strong taste? What is it? *(Child responds.)* That's salty salt. We put salt on food to flavor it. If our salt was not salty, it would be useless to put it on our food.

Jesus told his disciples, "You are the salt of the earth . . . and the light of the world" (Matt. 5:13-14 NLT). Do you think that means that as Christians we should hide and keep our belief in Jesus hidden so that it doesn't taste too strong to anyone? Should we be careful not to say anything about what we believe? *(Discuss with children.)*

Jesus wants us to be salty, and he wants us to shine brightly. People around us should know for sure that we're Christians. We should show them love and acceptance and tell them about God and invite them to church.

A little bit of salt on food can make a big difference. One little light can push back the darkness. Just a few salty Christians in a neighborhood can make a difference. Followers of Jesus can change entire neighborhoods, whole societies, even a country.

You are the salt of the earth and the light of the world, so be salty and shine brightly and give glory to God!

Help us to be salty Christians, Lord. May we shine brightly in our world and show others the way to you.

Notes

Choose Life

Preparation: Bring two signs, one with the word "Life" and the other with the word "Death" written in large letters.

A long time ago, God's chosen people, the Israelites, were traveling without a homeland. After forty long years of wandering through the wilderness and waiting, they were finally ready to enter the promised land. Moses was not able to go with them, so he had a serious talk with them before he left.

The Israelites were like children to Moses. He had been leading them and trying to give them everything they needed for so many years, it was as if he was their own father. But he finally had to say goodbye to them. Moses wanted them to be safe even if he couldn't be with them any longer, so he gave them a lecture. When all of you get older, you might hear the same sort of talk from your folks when you're ready to go live on your own or travel off to college.

Moses set two choices before the Israelites and told them that they must decide which path they wanted to take. Moses said, "See, I have set before you this day life and good, death and evil." Life or death; seems like a pretty easy choice to make. I brought along a couple of signs to remind you of the two choices. *(Hand "Life" sign to your right and have a child hold it up; hand "Death" sign to your left.)* Some of the choices that go along with "Life" are obeying and loving the Lord and keeping his commandments. Some of the choices that go along with "Death" are turning away from God and making other things more important in your life than God.

Well, that's an obvious choice, right? How many of you would choose life? Raise your hand. How many would choose death? It's easy to decide to take the right path when it's labeled so clearly like this, but really life is made up of many little choices. *(Give relevant examples here. Examples follow.)* Imagine that your mom or dad has just told you that you have to do the dishes or clean up your room. Suddenly, the doorbell rings, and it's your best friend. And your friend has a new toy that he wants to show you or a new video game that she wants to play with you. It would be very tempting to run off and play with them and forget about your job, but that would be disobeying your folks and that's a step down the wrong path.

Choosing to obey your parents is like choosing life; choosing to disobey is like choosing death. We make lots of little choices every day, and with Jesus' help, we can make the right choice and choose life.

Dear Jesus, help us to make the right choices and to follow your will for our lives.

Notes

7th Sunday after Epiphany   Matt. 5:38-48 and
                                                1 Cor. 3:18-19

An Eye for an Eye

**Preparation: Bring an organ donation card with you; your own or
one from a member of the congregation.**

Can anyone tell me what the word *revenge* means? *(Discuss meaning and examples of revenge with children.)* Revenge is getting back at someone who hurt you. In today's Gospel reading, Jesus talks about revenge. The people that Jesus was talking to knew about the old law that said, "'If an eye is injured, injure the eye of the person who did it. If a tooth gets knocked out, knock out the tooth of the person who did it'"(Matt. 5:38 NLT). Everyone accepted this law and thought it was fair.

But Jesus told them something very different. He told the people not to take revenge on those who hurt them. Jesus told them that if someone slapped them on one cheek, they were to turn the other cheek toward him and let him slap that one as well. Does that sound silly? If you hit back, does the fight continue and even get worse? Yes, it does. If you don't strike back, that is usually the end of the fight.

I want to tell you a true story about a little boy and his parents. They were a family from California who were on vacation in Italy. One day, a car pulled up alongside them and gunshots were fired into their car. The little boy, Nicholas, was sitting in the back seat and was killed. His parents were very sad. But they found a way to bring good out of this tragedy. They decided to donate Nicholas' organs to seven people.

Instead of wanting to take away someone's life to get revenge for their little boy, those parents gave life to seven people.

This act of forgiveness shocked the people of Italy. At that time, not very many people in Italy were willing to donate their organs after they died to others who needed them. Many people now have organ donor cards that they carry with their driver's license. If they have an accident and die, then important parts of their body can be used to help others live. If someone dies and donates their heart, then a doctor can put the healthy heart into a person who needs it.

As a way of showing their thanks for this gift of life from Nicholas and his parents, 130 bells were given by families, churches, and schools throughout Italy. These bells were hung on a tower that was built to honor the memory of Nicholas. Nicholas and his parents did what Jesus would have done. Instead of seeking revenge, they gave life.

Thank you Lord, for people of love and mercy. Help us to turn the other cheek; to turn away from revenge and to turn toward forgiveness and life.

Notes

Worrying Away Your Time

Preparation: Bring a one-minute timer. You may use a small sand hourglass or set a one minute alarm.

Do any of you have any worries? I know that I sometimes worry about things. To worry is to think about something that might happen that you don't want to happen. Or you may worry that something you really do want to happen won't ever happen. What do you or your family and friends worry about? Before we start listing our worries, let me set this one-minute timer, and we'll all talk about our worries for one minute. *(Set timer and then discuss worries with children.)*

We worry about lots of things, don't we? We worry about our classes in school and our homework. We worry about what we're going to wear and whether or not other people will think our clothes look nice. We worry about what we're going to fix for lunch. We just spent at least a minute worrying about things. Was that a minute added to our lives or subtracted from our lives? Did we gain a minute by worrying, or did we lose a minute? *(Let children respond.)* We really don't have anything to show for our worrying, do we? We probably could have done something better with that minute.

Jesus had some very important things to say about worry. Jesus said, "Don't worry about everyday life—whether you have enough food, drink, and clothes. Doesn't life consist of more than food and clothing? Look at the birds. They don't need to plant or harvest or put food in barns because your heavenly Father feeds them. And you are far more valuable to him than they are. Can all your worries add a single moment to your life? Of course not" (Matt. 6:25-27 NLT).

We don't add anything to our life by worrying. The time we spend worrying is wasted time. Do you think God already knows what you need? Yes, he does. And the Lord wants us to know that our minds should be on more important things than what we're going to wear or eat. We should be thinking about how to help others and how to tell people about Jesus' love.

Jesus also said, "Your heavenly Father already knows all your needs, and he will give you all you need from day to day if you live for him and make the kingdom of God your primary concern" (Matt. 6:32-33 NLT).

Dear Jesus, help us to be thinking about God's kingdom instead of wasting time worrying about the unimportant things of life. Thank you for providing for all of our needs.

Notes

Without a Doubt

Preparation: Bring a lamp or flashlight with a translucent shade that allows a little, but not all, of the light to show through. Have the light shining as you begin your talk.

D o you know what this Sunday is? It isn't Easter or Christmas, is it? No, but today we do celebrate a very important happening in Jesus' life. Today is Transfiguration Sunday. One day Jesus took three of his disciples away from the crowds that usually followed Jesus around and they went on a long hike. Those four friends hiked up a big mountain and when they got to the top of the mountain, do you know what happened?

Jesus was transfigured in front of those disciples. His face shone like the sun and his garments were glowing white. Do you think the disciples were surprised? They'd never seen Jesus like this; usually he looked ordinary and human just like them. And Jesus was human, but his disciples knew he was also special. They knew that he was God's own Son, the Savior of the world. But maybe they sometimes forgot just how powerful and amazing he was. Perhaps they doubted that he was the Son of God.

The disciples knew that Jesus was the Light of the world; he had told them so. They had seen in his life, words, and miracles, a glimpse of the glory of God. It was as if they were looking at a lamp with its light shaded from view, sort of like this lamp. *(Show lamp with shade.)* When Jesus was transfigured on the mountain, it's as if the shade was taken away and the disciples could see the true brightness of God's glory.

Well do you know what happened next? A bright cloud came over them and God's voice came from the cloud and said, "This is my beloved Son, and I am fully pleased with him. Listen to him" (Matt. 17:5 NLT). Do you think those disciples had any doubts about who Jesus was at that moment? There was no doubt about it. Jesus was God's Son. He was shining with heaven's glory; God was speaking. There was no doubt.

This Sunday we remember what happened on that mountain, and we know without a doubt who Jesus really is. He is God's own Son, the Savior of the world.

We praise you, Jesus, God's own son, the Savior of the world. Remind us every day of your power and your glory.

Notes

Sweet Temptation

Preparation: Bring wrapped candies to pass out.

This morning, I want to find out how strong all of you are. Do you think you are stronger than something about the size of an ant? Could you beat an ant in a wrestling match? *(Let children respond.)* I'm sure you could! How about a little beetle? Are you stronger than a beetle? Probably. Well, I've got something in my sack here that's about this big. *(Indicate with thumb and forefinger about one-half to one inch.)* Do you think you're stronger than something that big? Okay, I'll show you what I have. Candies!

No, I don't want you to have a wrestling match with candy. I don't want to see how strong these muscles are. *(Indicate biceps.)* I want to see how strong you are inside.

We're reading a lot of verses this Sunday about temptation. Does anyone know what temptation is? *(Let children answer.)* It's seeing something that you really want, but knowing that you should not take it, or wanting to do something that you know you shouldn't do. Has this ever happened to any of you? *(Listen to stories offered.)* I know it's happened to all of us grown-ups here. Temptation can be really tough to deal with. It's hard to resist. Sometimes we really need to pray to God and ask for help. "Please God help me from taking that candy!" or "Dear God, I'm really mad at my sister and I want to hit her. Please help me not to!" With God's help you can resist temptation.

Now I'm going to give everyone of you a little temptation; and I'm going to ask you to not unwrap it or eat it until after the service and your feet have stepped outside of this church building, then it's okay to eat it as long as your folks agree.

So while you're here in church, try to resist the temptation to eat it, because you're really not supposed to eat in church. You've got to wait. If you can wait, then you've won a small battle and you will be stronger! *(Hand out wrapped candies.)*

Now if you don't think you're strong enough, you can give your temptation to your folks to hold for you . . . that is as long as they're strong enough to resist it. Okay, the resistance army can march back to their pews now. Be strong in the Lord!

Lord, give us the strength to resist doing those things that we should not do.

Notes

Being Born Again

This morning, I'd like to know how many of you were born at least once? Raise your hand if you know, for sure, that you have been born once. Okay, now I want to know how many of you were born twice? That may sound like a silly question. Can a baby crawl back inside its mother after it has been born? *(Let children answer.)*

Nicodemus, who is mentioned in the Gospel reading for today, asked this same question of Jesus. Of course a baby can't be born again physically. Even if this were somehow possible, any mother who has been through labor would not allow this to happen! We were all born once when we came out of our mothers. What could the second birth be? *(A child may answer correctly.)* Yes! When you are baptized, you are born again.

Let's talk about the first kind of birth. It's a lot of work being born. It's difficult for both the mother and the baby. The mother is pushing with all her might. The baby's heart is beating hard as it's being born. But what a wonderful thing to finally make it out into the world and find arms to welcome you into a family that has been wanting you for so long!

Now the second kind of birth. It's God who does all the work. He died on the cross to take away all the bad things in us, all our sin. He made the sacrifice so that we could enter into his family. When we're baptized, we become children of God, and Christians all over the world are part of our family. Do you see all of the people here who came to church this morning? They are part of your family, the family of your second birth!

As you go back to your seats this morning, I'd like for us to do something to remind us that when we were baptized, we were born again as children of God into his family. I'd like two volunteers to be the birth doorway. *(Have two kids make an arch with their arms that the others can pass under.)* As you pass through this doorway on your way back to your seats, remember that in baptism, you were born again.

Father in heaven, thank you for welcoming us into the family of Christ through baptism. Thank you for our second birth.

Notes

Meanie in the Quicksand

Preparation: Bring a long, sturdy rope.

I want you to think about your friends this morning. Can you think of a lot of friends? Who are some of your friends? *(Allow children to give a few names.)* What is the opposite of a friend? *(Let children respond.)* An enemy is the opposite of a friend. I hope none of you have enemies at such a young age, but sometimes it seems like certain people are just hard to get along with. We may try really hard to be nice to them, but maybe nothing works and we might start to see them as an enemy.

Do you think God has any enemies? I'm sure God doesn't want anyone to be his enemy, but when people turn their backs on God and refuse to listen to him or obey him, they become, by their own choice, enemies of God. That's a very sad thing, isn't it?

Now, imagine for a minute that you're all in a jungle. Pretend you're on a field trip with your class. You're hiking along next to someone who has been mean to you the whole trip. This person has been pulling your hair, dropping bugs down your shirt, and saying mean things about you, and you've just about had enough. This person has become an enemy. Suddenly, this mean person steps into a pit of quicksand! At first he doesn't want any help. "Get away from me," he sneers, "I can get out by myself." But you know he can't, and you've got a sturdy rope with you, just like the one I have here. What do you think you would do? Would you save this enemy? It might be tempting to drop a few bugs on this person's head while he's stuck there. You might feel like saying, "Serves you right, you big meanie!" and then let him sink.

There's a Bible verse in Romans, chapter 5, that says, "But God showed his great love for us by sending Christ to die for us while we were still sinners (or enemies of God)" (v. 8 NLT; *parentheses by author*). God didn't wait until we were his friends to save us; he saved us while we thought of him as an enemy. That takes a lot of love, doesn't it?

We're all sinners. We all do things that we shouldn't do. In a way, we're all like that meanie, stuck in the quicksand. But even before we say, "Please, help me," God has already thrown us the rope and pulled us out. (*As you speak, you can throw one end of the rope out, or do the action of throwing a rope.*) God loves all of us and he sent Jesus to save us.

Dear Lord, thank you for saving us. Help us to be a friend of Jesus and help us to be a friend to those around us.

Notes

I Just Wanna Be a Sheep

Preparation: Bring cotton balls to represent sheep or make simple sheep from pom-poms to hand out to the children.

Does anyone know who King David was? He was king of Israel a long time ago. Do you know what he did before he became a king? He was a shepherd. A shepherd doesn't have a very glamorous job. He has to take care of a big flock of sheep. This is not easy, because sheep aren't very intelligent creatures. Almost every other farm animal you could name is smarter than a sheep.

So a shepherd has to show the sheep where they should eat grass, where they should drink fresh water, where they should lie down and go to sleep. The shepherd has to protect the sheep from hungry wolves and bears. He has to keep them from running off the edge of cliffs. He has to keep them from getting lost.

King David knew a lot about sheep. He knew how silly they were and how much they needed a shepherd. And after he became king, he wrote a song, a psalm, that begins, "The Lord is my shepherd" (Ps. 23:1 NLT). Now if the Lord is my shepherd, what does that make me? Right! A sheep! Isn't that insulting? No, just realistic. We do need God. We need taking care of. It would really be silly to think that we didn't need God as our shepherd. Do you think those sheep would last very long out in the wilderness without a shepherd? No!

I'd like to give each one of you a soft little sheep to remind you how sheep need a shepherd just like we need

God. Even though we're much smarter than sheep, in some ways we can be just as silly when we make bad choices and refuse to follow the Good Shepherd who loves us. *(You may pass out cotton balls and, if desired, teach the children a simple song.)*

I want to teach you a little song. Whenever you hear the word "sheep" you can say "Baa!" And when we're done, all of you little lambs can find your way back to your places.

Optional song, to the tune, "The Games People Play"

I just want to be a sheep (BAA!),
I just want to be a sheep (BAA!),
Pray the Lord my soul to keep,
I just want to be a sheep! (BAA!)

Dear Jesus, our good shepherd, thank you for watching over us and keeping us from harm.

Notes

Dry Bones

Preparation: Bring a model of a skeleton or a chicken bone as an illustration.

In the Old Testament reading today, Ezekiel describes a valley full of dry bones. This was a vision or dream that the Lord was showing to his prophet Ezekiel. It must have been quite a sight, a whole valley full of dry bones lying around. How do you think Ezekiel might have felt when he saw that? *(Let children share.)*

The Lord was showing this vision to Ezekiel for a very important reason. Those bones represented the Israelites, God's people, who had lost hope and had lost faith in God. Because they had turned so far from God, and had lost their spiritual life inside, they were like those lifeless bones.

Now if I gave you a skeleton of something like a chicken *(show your bone as an illustration)*, could you make that chicken alive again? Could you put the muscles and feathers back on the chicken and then make it start breathing again? *(Children may respond.)* That would be impossible for us, but for God, nothing is impossible. When Jesus was walking around here on earth, he raised people from the dead.

Ezekiel watched this valley of bones, and he spoke to the bones, just as the Lord told him to do. Do you know what happened to the bones right before his eyes? *(Children may answer.)* Those bones were connected back together and soon they had muscle and skin and they were human again. Then God breathed into them, and they stood up and were alive.

Ezekiel was given this dream to show him that God could do anything. The people of Israel were alive, but they felt very sad inside. They had stopped listening to God. It was as if their spirits were dead, like those dry bones. God sent the prophet Ezekiel to them to bring their hope and their spirits back to life.

Sometimes we feel sad and far away from God. We may feel like the Lord doesn't hear our prayers. We don't have to stay that way, far away from God like a dry bone. God wants us to be alive in him, full of the Holy Spirit and happy to be children of God. If we open our hearts and lives to him, the Spirit of God will come whooshing into our lives again.

Do you know what Jesus said to Mary and Martha before he raised their brother back to life? He said, "I am the resurrection and the life. Those who believe in me, even though they die . . . will live again" (John 11:25 NLT). Can you say the verse with me? *(Repeat with children.)*

Lord, we're thankful that you can do anything. Fill us with your Holy Spirit so that we will truly be alive in you.

Notes

A Noisy Parade

Preparation: Bring a large palm branch to signal the shouts of "Hosanna!" If possible, bring palm leaves to hand out to the children.

Today is Palm Sunday! Do you know what happened on Palm Sunday? There was a parade. How many of you have been to a parade? They're exciting to watch, aren't they? There are lots of people lining the streets, waiting to see the action. There's lots of noise; marching bands and horns; people yelling, laughing, and dancing; clowns throwing candy and kids running around. It's bright, colorful, and noisy.

I like parades. I want you to imagine that you're all sitting by the side of a dusty road, waiting for a parade to start. You got up early to get a good seat and you're waiting. You wait for a long time, but you don't hear anything. Finally you hear voices, shouting, singing, laughing. You see dust rising at the end of the road.

Someone's coming! First you see the people with palm branches, waving them around, and throwing them on the ground. Then you see colorful blankets thrown on top of the dust, making a tapestry path for someone important. Finally, you see the guest of honor, the King, making his triumphant entry into Jerusalem! You expect him to be riding in a fine chariot drawn by splendid horses, or at least in a fancy seat carried by servants. But that is not the way that this King arrived in Jerusalem. How did he make his entrance? (*Children may answer.*)

He came riding on a young donkey. Have you ever seen a parade that consisted solely of one man riding on a donkey? It may not sound that exciting, but this was King Jesus, the man who could do miracles and heal people. The crowd knew who he was, and they went wild! They yelled, waved palm branches, and threw their coats on the road! Did they make a lot of noise? They sure did! The whole city heard them! Everyone came running.

We're going to hand out these palm leaves for you to wave, and I'd like everyone on this side to yell, "Hosanna!" and everyone over here to yell, "Blessed are you, King Jesus!" When I raise this big palm branch, you can start yelling. If I raise it really high, you can yell really loud. When I lower the branch down, stop yelling, okay?

Let's see what Palm Sunday might have sounded like! *(Raise palm branch and encourage everyone, including grown-ups, to join in.)* Hosanna to the Lord! Hosanna in the highest!

Blessed are you, King Jesus. We honor you today as the Messiah and our Lord and Savior. Hosanna!

Notes

Surprise!

Preparation: Bring a carton of raw eggs and a bowl. One egg should be blown hollow and dry. Enlarge one of the openings and insert confetti. Cover the openings with white tissue and paraffin wax so that the hollow egg looks like the others.

Happy Easter, everyone! Have any of you ever been surprised? What surprised you? *(Wait for answers.)* When the disciples of Jesus went to the tomb that first Easter morning, were they surprised? Yes! They really were! They expected to find the body of Jesus lying there, but what did they find?

The cloths that had wrapped Jesus' body were lying there, but no Jesus. They were surprised! But they didn't have to be surprised. If the disciples had been listening carefully to Jesus earlier, they would have heard him say that he had to die and that three days later, he would rise again. He told them, but maybe it seemed too incredible to believe at the time.

It might be a little like telling you that if I crack this egg open *(take a normal egg out of carton)*, we'll find a colorful surprise. Everyone knows that inside a raw egg, there's a yolk and clear slimy stuff. I'll crack one now and show you. *(Crack egg over a bowl so that everyone can see.)* There's the inside of the egg; just what we expected. No surprise. The disciples knew from experience that when a person died and was buried in a tomb, that person stayed in the tomb. It was hard to believe that this time it would be different.

Now, I'm going to take an egg from the carton here *(make sure it's the confetti egg)*, and I'm going to tell you that this time it's going to be different. There's nothing slimy or wet in this egg. There's a colorful surprise inside that will appear when I break this egg. I know for sure that this is true. If you believe me, raise your hand.

Okay, would you come over here and let me crack this egg on your head? *(Have one of the believers stand up so everyone can see. Cover blow holes with fingers as you crack the egg and open it. Confetti will flutter down, which you can distribute to the children or sprinkle over their heads.)*

There was a good surprise inside that egg, wasn't there? What I told you was true. And what Jesus told the disciples was true. On the third day, the tomb of Jesus didn't contain death; out of the tomb came life. Jesus is alive! Hallelujah! I wish all of you many good surprises this Easter.

We praise you, risen Lord, for surprising your disciples and us by conquering death and bringing forgiveness and eternal life.

Notes

The Purpose of the Book

Preparation: Bring your Bible with verses marked and several how-to books, such as a car repair manual, calligraphy handbook, or cookbook.

I brought several books with me today that I wanted to show you. Each book was written for a specific reason. I'll show you each book and you see if you can figure out why the book was written. *(Present your how-to books and let children guess what their purposes are.)*

All of these books have a purpose: to teach the reader how to do something or to explain something. Of course, some books are written to entertain us, but even those books are bound to teach us something in the process.

Now, I have one more book to show you. This one is a best-seller. More copies of this book have been printed than any other book in the world. Do you know what book it is? *(Let children guess and then show them the book.)* It's the Bible.

Why was the Bible written? What is the purpose of this book? Was it written to explain in detail how the world was created? There are instructions for building an ark in here. Was it written to teach ship-building? If you were listening carefully to the Gospel reading this morning, you heard the answer.

The Gospel of John, chapter 20, tells about how Jesus appeared to one of the disciples, named Thomas, who had trouble believing that Jesus was really alive. This happened about a week after Easter. Jesus' disciples were together and Thomas was with them. The doors were shut, but Jesus appeared suddenly and stood with them. Jesus said to Thomas, "Put your finger here and see my hands. Put your hand into the wound in my side. Don't be faithless any longer. Believe" (John 20:27 NLT). And Thomas looked at Jesus and believed. And Jesus said to Thomas, "You believe because you have seen me. Blessed are those who haven't seen me and believe anyway" (John 20:29 NLT).

The Gospel goes on to say, "Jesus' disciples saw him do many other miraculous signs besides the ones recorded in this book. But these are written that you may believe that Jesus is the Messiah, the Son of God, and that by believing in him you will have life" (John 20:30-31 NLT).

Why were these things written? "So that you may believe that Jesus is the Messiah, the Son of God, and that by believing in him *you* will have life!" As you read and study your Bibles and listen to Bible stories, always remember the purpose of this book. It leads you to faith and to life.

Thank you, Lord, for giving us the Bible so that we might believe and have life.

Notes

Who Was That?

Preparation: You can begin the children's sermon by donning a pair of dark sunglasses or a fake nose and mustache and ask the children if they recognize you.

Can you recognize me? I'm wearing a disguise, but do you still know who I am? *(Let children answer.)* Today's Gospel lesson tells the story of how the disciples met Jesus on the day of his resurrection. The first time they saw Jesus, even though he wasn't wearing a disguise, they didn't recognize him!

The disciples had already been told by the two Marys who saw the empty tomb and the angels that Jesus wasn't dead; he was alive, but they still didn't believe it. They were walking to a town called Emmaus, sadly talking about how Jesus had died, when Jesus himself came walking right up alongside them and asked them what they were discussing. Did they recognize Jesus then? No! Has this ever happened to you? Have you ever not recognized someone that you know really well . . . maybe at Halloween, or at a costume party? *(Wait for answers.)* Well, Jesus wasn't in disguise, and they still didn't recognize him!

(Here you can tell your own story of not recognizing someone or elaborate on one of the children's stories. An example follows.) Quite a few years ago, I took a trip to North Dakota with a friend to visit some of his relatives and to help his uncle and cousin do some work on their farm. While we were there, they took a picture of me, wearing some borrowed clothes,

my hair pulled back, with an old baseball cap on my head. When I got home from the trip, I showed my dad the photos we took. We got to the picture of me and my dad asked, "And who is this guy?" I couldn't believe it! My own dad didn't recognize me. I strung him along for a while, saying that it was one of my friend's cousins and that people thought we looked a lot alike. Dad didn't think there was much resemblance. I finally told him that it was a photo of me and scolded him for not recognizing his own daughter!

Jesus' disciples didn't recognize him either, even though he talked with them for quite a while. They didn't expect to see Jesus at all at that time. It just didn't register that he was alive. He had told them he would be resurrected; the two Marys had told them; but they couldn't believe it. Then when he broke the bread at supper, a familiar and special action that they'd seen him do before he died, finally, they recognized him. They knew it was Jesus and they were very happy that he was alive!

Lord Jesus, help us to recognize your presence in our lives and welcome you always.

Notes

Shepherd and Door

Preparation (Optional): You can bring a picture of Jesus as the Shepherd or point out a picture in the church. Show your illustration after asking the children if they know who the Good Shepherd is. Pick your volunteer "wolf" out ahead of time.

W ho is the Good Shepherd? Can anyone tell me? *(Let children respond.)* Yes, Jesus is the Good Shepherd. *(You may show your illustration here.)* In the Gospel lesson read today, Jesus says, "I am the gate for the sheep" (John 10:7 NLT). So besides being a shepherd, Jesus is the door.

Did you know that in Bible times, a couple thousand years ago, being a door was part of a shepherd's job? The sheep pen was usually a stone wall built in a circle with only one opening. So after the shepherd had gathered all the sheep into the pen for the night, he would have to lie down across the opening to guard the sheep. The only way a wolf could get in was through that door, so the wolf would have to deal with the shepherd first. Do you think a good shepherd would let a wolf through that door? No sir! The shepherd would drive the wolf away!

Let's see if we can build a sheep pen here at the front of the church. I need some volunteers to be part of the wall. *(Choose some kids and help to arrange them.)* You stones sit here along the altar rail and don't move. You're part of the wall. We'll pretend that the wall goes all along the altar rail, so a wolf can't get in that way. We'll leave an opening here for the doorway.

Now the rest of you are sheep. It's getting dark, so you'd better get into the fold. You'll be safe there. Now, I need a good shepherd. The good shepherd comes over here and lies down in the doorway. The shepherd is the door to the sheep fold. It's a good thing too, because there's a big, scary-looking wolf out here who's on the prowl for a late-night snack of leg-of-lamb. See the wolf? *(Choose somebody from the congregation who would be willing to help.)*

The wolf is going to try to sneak past the shepherd without waking him up to get at the sheep. If the shepherd touches the wolf, then the wolf has to run away and the sheep are safe. *(Let players act it out.)*

Thank you, shepherd, for protecting the sheep. We can be thankful that Jesus is our Good Shepherd and that he always watches over us. We remember that Jesus gave up his own life to save us from sin and death.

Dear Jesus, you are the Good Shepherd. Thank you for keeping us in your care.

Notes

The Cornerstone

Preparation: Bring some building blocks and a bucket of stones.

Rocks and stones turn up in both of the lessons this morning and in the psalm that we read together. Stones were very important to the people in Jesus' time. Most of the buildings in the area where Jesus lived were made out of stone.

In 1 Peter, the Bible talks about Jesus being the cornerstone. Does anyone know what a cornerstone is? *(A child may answer correctly.)* The cornerstone is usually the largest stone in the building. It is placed first and the building rises around it. The cornerstone has to be strong with no hidden weaknesses or cracks in it, so that it can support the tremendous weight of the building.

The Bible also says, "And now God is building you, as living stones, into his spiritual temple" (1 Peter 2:5 NLT). So, if all of us in this congregation are living stones, making a spiritual temple or church, who do you suppose is our cornerstone? *(Wait for an answer.)* Yes, that's right. Jesus is our cornerstone, the most important part.

I brought some blocks with me today, and I thought we'd try a little experiment. We're going to construct a building. We can pretend these are stones, and this *(choose a large, long block)* is our cornerstone. We put the cornerstone down first, then start building around and on top of it. *(Construct a small building, making sure that the cornerstone is the essential element of its structural integrity.)*

Now, we've finished our building. What would happen, do you suppose, if we removed the cornerstone? *(Children may respond.)* Yes, it would probably fall down. Let's try it. *(Pull out the cornerstone, collapsing building.)* We need the cornerstone, don't we? And just as the church needs Jesus as its firm foundation, we need Jesus as the cornerstone of our lives. Without Jesus, everything falls apart.

I have here a bucket full of stones, and I'd like everyone to take one before you go back to your seats. As you hold the stones in your hands, remember that Jesus is your cornerstone.

Jesus, thank you for being the solid cornerstone in our lives. Your strength helps make us strong.

Notes

How Close Is God?

I f you could name something that is the farthest possible distance away from you, what would that thing be? What is something that is really far away from you? *(Discuss distant objects with children.)*

Now, if you could name something that is as close to you as is possible, what would that be? What are some things that are very, very close to you? *(Discuss close objects with children.)*

Some people think that God must live far away. If we could travel to go see God, how far do you think we'd have to go? If we thought that God lived somewhere in the "up" direction, and we got into a rocket ship to go and visit him, how far do you think our rocket would have to travel to finally get to where God is? *(Let children speculate.)*

But is God really far away from us? Does God live way out there in outer space? *(Children may answer.)* Our God is not a distant God. He wants to be right here with us. He sent his only son, Jesus, right here to our world to live with us and to die on the cross for us and to rise again to life. And when Jesus went up into heaven, he sent the Holy Spirit to fill every believer with the power of God.

God is close to us, isn't he? Jesus is closer than your mommy or daddy when they're hugging you tight; he's closer than a hug. Jesus is closer than our shoes and socks. He's closer than our skin. Acts, chapter 17, describes how close God is to us. The apostle Paul says, "he is not far from each one of us, for in him we live and move and have our being . . ." (Acts 17:27-28 RSV). God is so close that he's a part of us.

But Jesus only comes close to us if we allow him to. When we invite Jesus into our heart and accept him as our Savior and Lord, he does become a part of us. "In him we live and move and have our being."

So the next time you get a nice squooshy hug from someone, remember that Jesus is even closer than a hug! When you go back to your places, give someone a big hug and tell them how close Jesus is to them.

Lord Jesus, when we feel like you are far away, help us to remember how close you really are.

Notes

What Goes Up

Preparation: Bring one helium-filled balloon, preferably white. You may attach a long string to it if you wish to retrieve it after the service. Beware of obstacles, such as ceiling fans, during the sermon.

Today is the last Sunday of Easter in the church year. The white cloths on the altar will be taken down and replaced with red ones next Sunday. During this last week of Easter, the church celebrates the Ascension of Christ. Does anyone know what *ascension* means? *(Child may answer correctly.)* It means going up or rising. This balloon that I'm holding is trying to ascend.

That is just what Jesus did, he ascended. After his resurrection, Jesus appeared to his disciples at different times for about a month. He told them that he would be going home to heaven, returning to the Father, and that the Holy Spirit would come to them.

If I let this balloon go, it will rise up, won't it? Will it ever come back down? Eventually, it will . . . you know the saying, "What goes up, must come down." The helium inside eventually seeps out and the balloon comes back down. If I let it go now, does anyone know exactly when it will drift back down again? No we don't know for sure.

Jesus also told his disciples that he would be back someday. He didn't tell them when, but he promised to return.

Have you ever lost a balloon, or seen someone let go of one? They'll stand there watching the balloon go up and up until they can't see it anymore. If it's a little child who has lost the balloon, there may be some tears.

When Jesus went up into heaven, his disciples were watching. They watched him disappear into a cloud and then they all just stood there, looking up, staring at the sky, until two angels appeared and told them that Jesus would come back some day. The disciples were probably very sad to see Jesus go, and I'm sure they couldn't help standing there, staring for a while. Do you think they were supposed to just stay there, looking up, waiting for Jesus to come back? No, there was plenty to do while they waited for Jesus to return. The world was waiting to hear the good news, that Jesus was alive!

We can let this balloon go, watch it rise up, and probably sometime during the next few days it will float down. Now when you look at that balloon, remember that while we wait for Jesus to return, we can tell people the good news.

Thank you Jesus, for your promise that one day you will return. While we wait, help us to spread the good news of your love.

Notes

Many Gifts, One Spirit

Preparation: Bring little red cards, cut to look like flames, with a tag on the back of each one describing a gift of the Holy Spirit or a talent that one might be given to serve God.

Today is a very important birthday. Do you know whose birthday it is? *(Let children guess.)* Today we celebrate Pentecost Sunday, the birthday of the Christian church. Before Jesus was born, were there any Christian churches? No. There were Jewish synagogues where God's people, the Israelites, went to worship. Jesus taught in the synagogues while he was here on earth.

After Jesus died and rose from the dead, he told his disciples that although he would be returning to the Father in heaven, they would not be left all alone. Jesus promised them that the Holy Spirit would be sent down to remain with them and in them. God would always be with them. They just had to wait for the Holy Spirit to come down.

And what God has promised, God delivers! On the day of Pentecost, all the disciples were gathered together and there was the sound of a rushing wind and over every disciple's head, a flame appeared. The Holy Spirit filled every person in the room, and they began preaching the Gospel in many different languages. The Holy Spirit came, just as Jesus had promised. That was the birthday of the Christian church.

The first birthday of the church sounds like it was a very exciting day. Do you think there was a cake with candles on it? *(Children may respond.)* They didn't have a cake, but there were flames, weren't there? Over the disciples' heads, there were flames to show that the Holy Spirit was there. I brought some red paper flames with me this morning. I'll give each one of you a flame to take with you. *(Distribute paper flames.)*

At a birthday, we often have candles lit on the cake. What else do you have at a birthday? *(A child may answer correctly.)* We give gifts, don't we? Were gifts given on that first birthday of the church? Yes! The Holy Spirit gave gifts to the disciples then and the Holy Spirit gives gifts to us today. On the back of the flame I gave you, something has been written. It describes a gift or a talent that God might give to someone so they can help others and serve the Lord. Does someone want to read out loud one of the gifts? *(Let children share.)*

It's important to remember that one gift is not better than another. All of the gifts and talents are important in God's family. Treasure the gifts that God has given to you!

We remember the birthday of your church, Lord, and we thank you for the gifts of the Holy Spirit that you have given to your people. Help us to use those gifts to your glory.

Notes

In Charge

Preparation (Optional): You may bring along some small paper garbage bags to hand out.

Can anyone tell me the first words that you read in the Bible? *(Wait for answer.)* Genesis 1:1 reads, "In the beginning God created the heavens and the earth" (RSV). The first chapter of the Bible then goes on to describe the creation of everything in the heavens and on the earth. Can you tell me some of the things that God created? *(Let children respond.)* That's right. God created everything.

What did God create last of all? *("People," may come as response.)* Yes. God created man and woman. Genesis 1:26 reads, "Then God said, 'Let us make (people) in our image, after our likeness; and let them have dominion over the fish of the sea, and over the birds of the air, and over the cattle, and over all the earth, and over every creeping thing that creeps upon the earth'" (RSV).

God wanted people to have dominion over all the earth. Do you know what the word "dominion" means? It means to have authority over something, to be in charge; it's something like being a king or a queen of a country. Trying to be a good ruler or a president of a country must be a tough job. It's even a bigger challenge to be in charge of the whole earth.

I want you to imagine that you are the ruler of a small forest. It has a quite a few trees, lots of shrubs and flowers, and right in the middle of the forest, there is a beautiful pond where the animals go to drink. You are in charge of all the animals and plants and insects in this forest. It's up to you to make sure that all your subjects are healthy and happy and well cared for. Do you think that you would let somebody throw trash in your forest? Would you let anyone pour something like motor oil into the little pond? Would you pick all the flowers in your forest, until there weren't any left? *(Discuss with children.)* You would protect your creatures, wouldn't you? You would want to take good care of your forest and keep it healthy.

We humans sometimes forget, however, that we're in charge of the earth. We need to protect the animals, plants, and insects that God created. God gave us dominion; he put us in charge. It's a big job, and I hope we all remember to take good care of God's creation. *(At this point, you may hand out small garbage bags and remind children and parents to pick up any trash or litter that they might see today.)*

Dear God, please bless the animals great and small and help us to care carefully for all of your wonderful creation.

Notes

Nothing to Brag About

ave any of you ever played a game in which the other person let you win? *(Let children answer and give examples.)* Some games are really hard to learn and an older person has to spend some time teaching you. *(Here you may give an example of a game that was taught to you when you were a child. An example follows.)*

When I was little, my dad taught me how to play chess. It's a complicated game; each playing piece moves in a different way than the others. The king can move one space in any direction. The queen can move as far as she can in any direction. And pawns can usually only move one or two spaces forward. It took quite a while for me to learn the game well enough to play a full game, so to start me off, my dad would remove several of his own pieces to give me a head start. Then it was possible for me to win, but I didn't really win on my own. My dad helped me.

When someone is playing a game with you and they let you win, should you brag and say that you won all by yourself? *(Let children respond.)* It's not true that you did it by yourself, is it? The person helping you actually won for you. You really don't have anything to brag about.

Getting forgiveness for our sins and reaching heaven at the end of our lives is much more important than just playing a game. But like being allowed to win a game when we're little, it is what God does that allows us to be forgiven and to gain eternal life.

In Romans, chapter 3, the Bible says, "For all have sinned; all fall short of God's glorious standard" (v. 23 NLT). So none of us are at the finish line; none of us has won. Then it says, "Yet now God in his gracious kindness declares us not guilty. He has done this through Christ Jesus who has freed us by taking away our sins" (v. 24 NLT). God has won the battle against sin and death by sending Jesus to die for us. We have only to believe that as the truth to be forgiven and saved.

So even though we're saved and we've won the battle against evil, do we have anything to brag about? No; it is God who did it all for us because he loves us and wants us to win eternal life.

Dear mighty and loving God, thank you for winning the battle for us. Thank you for sending your son, Jesus, to die on the cross to take away our sin. We believe in you and what you have done for us.

Notes

Visiting the Doctor

D o you go to a doctor when you're well or when you're sick? *(Wait for answer.)* Nowadays, we may see the doctor for a check-up once or twice a year, even when we feel fine. But in Jesus' day doctors were only seen for emergencies, when someone was very sick or badly injured. Healthy people didn't go to the doctor, only sick people. In the Gospel reading today, Jesus says, "Healthy people don't need a doctor—sick people do" (Matt. 9:12 NLT).

The reason Jesus said this is that some Pharisees saw Jesus and his disciples having supper with people that they didn't approve of. They were the type of people that the Pharisees thought were pretty rotten.

The Pharisees were very careful to follow all the rules, and they went to church a lot and prayed loudly in the streets. The people that Jesus was eating with didn't go to church, didn't pray aloud or read scripture every day, and they sometimes cheated other people out of their money. Nobody in their neighborhood liked them. The Pharisees asked the disciples, "Why does your teacher eat with tax collectors and sinners?" (Matt. 9:11 RSV).

And Jesus answered them himself, "Healthy people don't need a doctor—sick people do. . . . I have come to call sinners, not those who think they are already good enough" (Matt. 9:12-13 NLT). If Jesus is the doctor, who do you think is going to go see him? The people who think that there is nothing at all wrong with them, those who figure they're doing everything right and don't need a savior? No! People who know that they make mistakes and do bad things, those who know that they need forgiveness are the ones who go to Jesus!

Do you think there really are people that never do anything wrong and really have no need to be forgiven? Are there people who don't need Jesus? *(Discuss this with children.)* There are people who don't think they need Jesus, but the truth is that we *all* need Jesus. We all need forgiveness, every one of us. Jesus heals our sin-sick souls with his forgiving love. He makes our spirits well, so that we're healthy and healed on the inside.

Lord Jesus, we need your healing touch in our lives. Thank you, Jesus, for loving us and forgiving us every day.

Notes

The Time Is Ripe

Preparation: Bring a basket of fruit.

Have you ever seen a tree that has fruit lying on the ground beneath it? Seeing that fruit just lying there, what does it make you feel like doing? *(Wait for answer "pick it up" or "eat it.")* If you're like me, it makes you want to pick it up. That fruit is ripe and it would go to waste if it was just left there on the ground. But you probably should go ask the owner of the tree if it would be all right to pick up some of the fruit. I brought a basket of fruit with me this morning. I bought it at the grocery store, but I brought it along to help us talk about harvesting. *(Optional: Bring something you harvested yourself.)*

In Matthew, chapter 9, Jesus tells his disciples, "The harvest is so great, but the workers are so few. So pray to the Lord who is in charge of the harvest; ask him to send out more workers for his fields" (vv. 37-38 NLT). Jesus isn't really talking about picking ripe apples or gathering wheat, he's talking about preaching the good news. Jesus could see that there were many people ready to hear that God loves them and not enough people to tell the good news. It was as if Jesus were looking out over a huge field of wheat that was just ready to be harvested. If no one came to gather the wheat into the barn, all that wheat would be wasted. Jesus tells the disciples to pray that more people would come forward to help with the harvest, to tell others about God.

If Jesus had told his disciples today that the harvest was plentiful, but there weren't enough workers, one of the disciples may have suggested simply using a big tractor to harvest that field in very little time. Do you think telling people about God works like that? Using a tractor would be like putting a big speaker on a truck and driving through the streets announcing to all that could hear that God loves them. Some people might listen, but I'm sure they'd be more likely to listen to someone they know, like a friend.

If we had a big apple tree growing right in the middle of church and there were lots of ripe apples hanging in the tree, I'm sure all of you would do a good job of harvesting those delicious apples. Some of you could climb way up into the branches and get the apples growing way up high.

I think all of you could be good laborers for God. When you tell your friends about Jesus, you're helping to bring in a harvest. Before you go back to your seats, please come and get a piece of fruit out of the basket.

Help us to be good workers, Lord, and tell others the good news.

Notes

The Hairs on Your Head

Preparation: Arrange for one of the children to bring their father up to the front to answer the questions. (This sermon also works well for Father's Day.)

This morning, I would like to ask a parent some questions about one of his or her children sitting up here. I want to ask things like their name, age, favorite food. Are there any volunteers? *(You may interview a volunteer or someone that you have previously arranged to help out.)* This will be a fairly short interview.

Is your child a girl or a boy? How many fingers does she have? What is your daughter's name? How old is she? When's her birthday? What's one of her favorite foods? Does she have a favorite color? What does she like to do? What time did she wake up this morning? Can you tell me what she dreamed last night? What is she thinking right now? Exactly how many hairs does she have growing on her head?

The questions started out being pretty easy to answer, didn't they? Some of the questions could have been answered by someone who didn't know this person very well, but other questions could only be answered by a good friend or a parent, someone who really knows this person.

What questions couldn't be answered? *(Let children respond.)* She might have told someone what she dreamed last night, but it would be pretty difficult to know what someone was thinking without asking them. And it would take a long time to count how many hairs were growing on her head. Who do you think knows us even better than our parents or our best friends? *(Wait for answer.)* God knows everything about us, doesn't he?

In Matthew, chapter 10, it says, "The very hairs on your head are all numbered" (v. 30 NLT). God knows how many hairs each one of you have on your head. That's a pretty small detail, isn't it? Your family and friends know a lot about you, both good and bad, and they love you so much for who you are. There's no one in the whole world like you. God knows even more about us—every thought, every wish—and he loves us more than we can imagine.

The next time you brush your hair, I want you to remember that God cares about every little detail in your life, right down to the number of hairs on your head.

Lord God, you know us so well and still you love us. Help us to love others as you love us.

Notes

Inviting Jesus

Preparation: Make a large invitation card, inviting Jesus to have supper at your house.

I brought something with me this morning. Can you see what it is? *(Show the card around.)* It's an invitation. Can someone read who the invitation is made out to? *(Let one of the children read the card.)* That's right, I want to send this invitation to Jesus. And what is it an invitation for? *(Have "invitation to supper" written on the card.)* Yes! I want to invite Jesus to have supper at my house tonight at 6:00.

How do you think I should send this invitation to Jesus? How can I make sure that he'll get it? *(Let children come up with their own ideas.)* It's going to be pretty hard to deliver this invitation to heaven, but there is a way I can invite Jesus to dinner. The answer is in the Bible.

Jesus sent his disciples out into the world to tell everyone the good news about God's love. But before they left, Jesus gathered them together to tell them some important things. In Matthew, chapter 10, Jesus said to his friends, "Anyone who welcomes you is welcoming me, and anyone who welcomes me is welcoming the Father who sent me" (v. 40 NLT). Jesus also said, "And if you give even a cup of cold water to one of the least of my followers, you will surely be rewarded" (v. 42 NLT).

Jesus told his disciples that whoever welcomes or invites them, welcomes Jesus. So how could I invite Jesus to my house? *(A child may answer.)* I can invite one of Jesus' disciples, one of his friends, to my house. How many disciples or friends of Jesus do you see here? Raise your hand if you are a friend of Jesus!

There are a lot of disciples here, aren't there? Do you think you would be able to invite Jesus to your house? *(Let children respond.)* Yes, you could. When you invite one of Jesus' friends into your home, it's as if you are inviting Jesus himself. So now we all know how to give an invitation to Jesus, and we don't even have to travel all the way to heaven to get it to him!

Jesus, we invite you into our hearts and lives. Help us to serve you by opening our hearts and homes to others.

Notes

Crossed Wires

Preparation: Bring a robot, a robotic arm, or a picture of a robot as a visual aid.

H as anyone here ever seen a robot, or had the chance to operate a robotic arm? *(Let children comment. Option to show visual aid here.)* Robots are very reliable as long as they're assembled correctly. If you push the button marked forward, the robot will go forward. If you push a lever to guide a robotic arm to the right, it will go right. What would happen, though, if someone made a mistake in putting the robot together? What if a couple of wires got crossed and, when the robot was ready to go, it didn't work quite right? You push the button marked "Stand," and the robot sits. You push the button marked "Sit," and the robot stands. You realize something is wrong, so you push the button marked "Stop," and the robot takes off running and you never see it again. That would be bad, wouldn't it?

There are a couple of verses in Romans, chapter 7, that read, "I don't understand myself at all, for I really want to do what is right, but I don't do it. Instead, I do the very thing I hate. . . . When I want to do good, I don't. And when I try not to do wrong, I do it anyway" (v. 15, 19 NLT). Does this sound at all familiar? You're playing with your brother or with a friend, and you're trying to share and play nicely, but then suddenly he has something you want, or he does something you don't like and some very angry words jump right out of your mouth before you can stop them. Or your hand shoots out and you find that you've just hit somebody. This is not what you had in mind when you first started playing. You don't invite someone over to yell at him or hit him, you invite him over to play and have fun. It's almost as if there are some wires crossed inside and you can't stop yourself from doing things you don't want to do.

We're not robots, though, are we? We can't blame our mistakes on crossed wires. We can't claim that someone assembled us the wrong way. We're children of God, and we want to do the right thing, but sometimes we make mistakes. Sometimes we do just the opposite of what we want to do.

So what do you think we can do when we feel like doing something that we know is wrong? *(Let children suggest answers.)* Jesus is the one who can uncross our wires. He can set us free from doing things that we hate. The next time you feel like you're about to do something you know you shouldn't, ask for help. Ask Jesus to help you do the right thing.

Lord, forgive us for our sins and for doing things that we know are wrong. Help us to act the way that we know we should.

Notes

The Parable of the Sower

Preparation: Bring a big blanket or quilt.

The Gospel lesson for today is a wonderful story, and I thought it would be fun to act it out. Could you help me tell the story? I'll need hungry birds, the bright sun, tough thorns, and some seeds.

Who would like to be a hungry bird? You birds stand over here. *(Place birds stage right.)* Who would like to be the bright sun? *(Place sun at center.)* Who wants to be the tough thorns? *(Place thorns stage left.)* And will the rest of you be my seeds? You seeds stand next to me. This big blanket will be the good soil. We'll spread it out down here in the middle.

This is a story that Jesus told to a huge crowd of people, and it is called "The Parable of the Sower." A sower is someone who plants seeds. Many of the people in the crowd listening to Jesus were farmers. They knew a lot about seeds and soil and planting, so they were very interested in this story. I'm going to tell the story and play the part of the sower and together we can act it out.

(Here you may paraphrase the parable of the sower, adding your own words and actions as needed. An example follows.) A sower went out to sow. And as he sowed, some seeds fell along the path. I'm going to move these seeds over that way. *(Guide seeds stage right, over by birds. Continue with the story, guiding children in acting it out.)*

Thank you for acting out the story with me. Let's all gather on the good soil here and listen to what this story means. The seeds are the good news about Jesus Christ. Some people hear the good news, but before they get around to really thinking about it and understanding it, Satan comes like a big hungry bird and snatches it away.

Others may hear about Jesus and get really excited, but if trouble comes along like a blazing hot sun, they may decide that they really don't believe in Jesus after all, and their faith seeds just wither away.

Then there are some people who want to give their lives to Jesus, but so many other things spring up around them like choking thorns; things like money, new clothes, cool toys, and expensive cars. Those things, like the thorns, take over until there's no room left for the seeds of Jesus to grow.

And, thankfully, there are the seeds that fall on the good soil. Those are the folks who hear the good news and believe in Jesus with all their heart and they love the Lord for the rest of their lives.

Lord help us to be good soil and to love and serve you all of our lives.

Notes

Weeds in the Field

W hen Jesus talked to the crowds of people that gathered to hear him, he often taught them stories called parables. Jesus once told a parable comparing the kingdom of heaven to a field that had been planted with good seeds. The seeds sprouted and wheat came up, but something else sprouted with the wheat that no farmer would want in their field. What do you think that was? *(Wait for response.)* Weeds came up, right alongside the good plants.

The field workers wanted to pull those weeds out right away, but the master of the field stopped them. The wheat and the weeds were growing right next to each other and their roots were probably all mixed up together. What might happen if you tried to pull a full grown weed out and its roots were wrapped around the roots of a good plant right next to it? *(Wait for answer.)* The weed could pull the good plant right out with it! So the owner of the field told the workers to wait and let the good and bad plants grow up together. Then at harvest time, the weeds would be collected and burned, but the wheat would be gathered up.

The disciples knew this wasn't just a story about a field with weeds, and they wanted Jesus to tell them the meaning. So Jesus told them that the field represented the world and he was the owner of the field. Who do you think the good seeds are? I can see many good seeds from where I'm sitting. Those who love Jesus are the good seeds. Are there any bad seeds in our world? Yes, unfortunately there are people who do not love God and who do mean things to other people.

Saving the Ants

Do all the good people live in one part of the world and all the bad people live in another part? No, we're all mixed together. God's children live right next to people who don't love God. And even inside of a child of God, there may be some bad thoughts right along with all of the good thoughts.

I've often wondered why God just doesn't make all the people who do really bad things just disappear? But it isn't that simple. Do bad people sometimes change? They certainly do. Many chapters of our Bible were written by Paul, someone who hated Christians at first, and then his life changed and he began preaching the good news of Jesus to everyone.

Jesus said that at the end of the world, however, everything will be sorted out. The good will be gathered into heaven to be with Jesus. In the meantime, we can tell the good news of Jesus' love to those who are still trying to decide.

Help us to spread the good news of your love, dear Jesus, while we wait for you to return. May we reach out with the hand of love to those who have turned away from you.

Notes

Inseparable

Preparation: Bring with you a stuffed animal, preferably one that means something to you.

D o any of you have a favorite stuffed animal that you play with all the time? *(Let children tell about their favorites, then introduce your stuffed animal.)* I brought my favorite stuffed animal with me this morning. This is my bear, Winnie the Pooh. *(Here, you can tell your own story. An example follows.)* One Christmas morning, when I was four years old, I opened a big box and looked inside. There were all my friends from the Winnie the Pooh books! Kanga and Roo, Eeyore, Tigger and Piglet, and, of course, Pooh Bear. Winnie the Pooh was my favorite. I took him everywhere with me.

Now I want to read you a Bible verse from Romans, chapter 8. "I am convinced that nothing can ever separate us from (God's) love. Death can't, and life can't. The angels can't, and the demons can't. Our fears for today, our worries about tomorrow, and even the powers of hell can't keep God's love away. Whether we're high above the sky or in the deepest ocean, nothing in all creation will ever be able to separate us from the love of God" (vv. 38-39 NLT).

Can anything pull us away from God? No! We're inseparable. When I read this verse, I thought of my favorite stuffed animal and of other kids with their favorite toys. Have you ever seen someone try to take a favorite toy away from a child? They will hang on for all they're worth.

I imagined someone trying to take my Pooh Bear away from me. I really don't think anybody could manage it. I want you to try to take my favorite bear out of my arms, okay? When I say, "Go!" anyone can try to get my bear. Ready, GO! *(Hang on tightly to your stuffed animal. If needed, hold it high over your head.)* You couldn't take my favorite bear away from me because Pooh Bear and I are inseparable.

Think about how tightly you can hold your stuffed animals and how tightly you can hug the people that you love even more than your toys. God holds us closer than that. There is nothing on earth or in heaven that can take God away from us. Nothing, not even death, can pull us away from our heavenly Father's arms.

Tonight, as you give someone a big hug goodnight or when you snuggle down with your favorite stuffed animal held tight in your arms, remember that God holds us even closer, and he will never let us go.

Thank you, Almighty God, for holding us so close that nothing can ever take you away from us.

Notes

Come to the Waters

H ave you ever been to a state fair or a big festival where there are booths selling food of every kind? Sometimes the people working in the booths will yell out to those passing in the street and try to get some more customers. "Hot dogs! Foot-long hot dogs! Come and get your hot dogs!" or "Ice-cold snow cones! Satisfy your thirst! Lemon, strawberry, grape! Get your snow cones here!" Let's say you smell something that you really like and you go over to a booth all set to eat your favorite treat. You place your order and then reach into your pocket to pay, but you realize that you have no money. Do you think the people in the booth would give you the food anyway? Probably not. You need money to buy food at the fair.

There's a passage in Isaiah that sounds just like someone shouting from a booth at the fair. It reads, "Every one who thirsts, come to the waters; and he who has no money, come, buy and eat! Come buy wine and milk without price" (Is. 55:1 RSV). There's something different about this vendor, however. What's the difference? *(Children may answer.)* That's right! You don't need money at this booth. They're giving away free refreshment!

If you've ever gone to a state fair, you might find a milk stand where you could get all the milk you could drink for just a few cents. There might be a huge, shiny milk truck parked there that keeps the milk ice cold. It's wonderful to stand and drink glass after glass of cold milk on a hot day. That is a good deal, but it still costs money.

One place at the state fair in Minnesota that offered refreshment at no charge was a building that had chilled water and a cool place to sit and relax. There was a sign on the front that had that very same Bible verse from Isaiah on it. "Everyone who thirsts, come to the waters . . ." This building was run by church groups and as they gave people water to quench their thirst, they also gave them refreshment for their souls. They handed out fliers that told them of Jesus' love and invited them to come to church.

The most valuable thing offered at the fair turned out to be something that no amount of money could buy. It was free. There is nothing that we can do or say or pay to earn God's love. He gives it to us for free. You can drink a glass of water on a hot day, and be refreshed. But after an hour or so, you'll be thirsty again. The water of life and the bread of life which Jesus offers to us takes away the thirst and hunger of our souls. His love is all that we need.

Lord, we come to the waters of your love with thirsty souls. Thank you for the free gift of your love that refreshes and satisfies us completely.

Notes

Beautiful Feet

Preparation: Make award ribbons with foot-shaped medallions or medals with footprints on them to hang around each child's neck. Assemble a small panel of "judges" prior to the sermon.

This morning, I thought we could have a beauty contest. This will be different than most beauty contests because we're not going to be looking at faces or hair or how gracefully you walk. We're going to look at feet. Is there anyone willing to show me their feet? *(Let children who are willing show their feet, with or without shoes on. You may show your own feet.)* Let's line up all of our contestants and look at their feet. All of you have beautiful feet! This is going to be hard to judge.

While deciding the winner, I want to read something to you from Romans, chapter 10. "For 'Anyone who calls on the name of the Lord will be saved.' But how can they call on him to save them unless they believe in him? And how can they believe in him if they have never heard about him? And how can they hear about him unless someone tells them? And how will anyone go and tell them without being sent? That is what the Scriptures mean when they say, 'How beautiful are the feet of those who bring good news!'" (vv. 13-15 NLT).

Do you know why it says that those who tell others about Jesus have beautiful feet? During the time when the New Testament was written, if you had a message to deliver to someone, how could you get it to them? Could you telephone them or send the message by e-mail? No. They didn't have anything like that back then. If you wanted to deliver an important message to someone far away, you gave it to a messenger and he or she carried the message as fast as possible to deliver it. When a runner arrived with the news, especially if it was good news, they would be greeted with a soothing foot washing, a good meal, and a refreshing rest. A messenger who brought good news had beautiful feet.

Do you think that pastors at all churches have beautiful feet? Yes, they do. They are messengers of the good news of Jesus Christ, and they bring this message to many people. Do you tell other people about Jesus? If you do, then you have beautiful feet, too! Should we see if the judges have reached their decision? *(Go to "judges" and get medals ready.)*

The judges have decided that you all have beautiful feet and that all of you can do a wonderful job of telling others about Jesus. Come and get a "beautiful foot" medal before you go back to your seats.

Give us all beautiful feet, Lord, and make us swift and strong to carry the good news of your love to people everywhere.

Notes

You Are What You Speak

Preparation: Bring a box of animal crackers, enough for at least one cracker per child.

an someone tell me what's inside this box? *(Hold up the box of animal crackers and let the children respond.)* Yes, there are animal crackers inside. What sorts of animals do you think you would find in here? *(Let children offer animal names.)*

I'm going to open this box and pick out one cracker. *(Your examples can come from the crackers you pick. Some examples follow.)* Here's a lion. If I ate this lion, do you think I would start acting like a lion? Would I roar? No, of course not. I would still be me. If I ate an elephant cracker, would I turn gray and leathery and start trumpeting loudly? No! The things I eat don't make me who I am.

There's a saying, "You are what you eat." And that's sort of true, in a way. If you eat healthy food, you will most likely be healthy. But you don't actually turn into what you eat, do you? Can people ever tell if you're a mean person or a kind person by what you eat? Can they tell if you're a Christian by what you eat? *(Children may answer.)* No, not really.

Many years ago, when Jesus was preaching here on earth, there was a group of people called the Pharisees who had strict rules that told them what they could eat and when. They couldn't eat meat on certain days of the week. They had lots of rules about washing, especially before eating. One day when Jesus was talking to a large crowd, he said something that the Pharisees didn't like. He said, "It is not what goes into the mouth that defiles or makes a person sinful, but it is what comes out of the mouth that defiles or makes sinful." *(Paraphrase by the author.)*

Jesus was saying that you aren't what you eat, but you are what you speak. If you don't wash your hands before you eat, that doesn't make you a bad person. Or if you eat a mean-looking rhinoceros animal cracker, you don't become mean yourself. How can you tell if a person is mean or not? Do you watch what they eat or do you listen to what they say? *(Let children answer.)* Right! You can tell a mean person by mean words that come out of his or her mouth. If someone has Jesus in their heart, you'll usually hear them speak good, helpful, wonderful words.

So you can have a lion in your tummy, but remember that Jesus is in your heart and you are what you speak. *(Hand out animal crackers to children.)*

Live in our hearts, Lord Jesus, and help us to speak good and helpful words of love.

Notes

Jesus Is the Rock

Preparation: Bring a box of large rocks that can be knocked together without chipping or crumbling.

D o any of you collect rocks? *(Let children respond.)* I brought a rock collection along this morning. These are all rocks that I like for one reason or another. I'll show you some of them. *(Show your rocks and talk about them.)*

Isaiah, chapter 51, talks about rocks. It says, "Listen to me, all who hope for deliverance—all who seek the Lord! Consider the quarry from which you were mined, the rock from which you were cut!" (v. 1 NLT). Does anyone know what a quarry is? *(A child may offer an answer.)* It's a place where you get rocks. If you want to get granite, you have to go to a granite quarry. If you want sandstone, you have to go to a sandstone quarry. Could you get sandstone from a granite quarry? No, not very likely. The two kinds of rocks are formed in very different ways and are found in different areas.

When it says, "Consider the quarry from which you were mined, the rock from which you were cut," the prophet Isaiah is reminding God's people to remember their ancestors, Abraham and Sarah, and how they trusted in God and in his promises. God's people came from that family of faith, like rock comes from a quarry. Abraham and Sarah are our faith ancestors, too. They put their trust in God.

God's promises are dependable and solid, like rock. There are a lot of hymns about Jesus being the solid rock on which we stand. It is a good way to describe Jesus. He's solid. He doesn't get washed away by trouble or time. Jesus has promised that he will always be with us, and he *is* always with us.

To celebrate Jesus being our rock, this morning I thought we could have some rock music. Would all of you like to be a part of our rock band? I'd like some of you to take two rocks and knock them together. Those are your instruments. The rest of you can clap your hands while you sing the chorus. The part I'll be singing is pretty simple, too, and everyone can join in as soon as they feel like it. Ready? Let's rock!

Jesus is my rock, and he rolls my blues away;
Bop shoo bop, shoo bop, whoo. *(Repeat 3 times.)*
(Repeat song several times, inviting kids to clap and congregation to join in.)
Thank you. You make an excellent rock band.

Everlasting God, you are our solid rock, and we put our trust in you.

Notes

15th Sunday after Pentecost Jer. 15:16 and
Rom. 12:21

Sweet Words

Preparation: Pour a box of alphabet-shaped cereal into a bowl to distribute at the end of sermon, or prepare small bags of cereal to give to each child.

Have you ever thought about how words would taste if you could eat them? Some words really sound like the thing they describe, don't they? The word *soft*, for example, sounds soft. But if you could taste the word *soft*, what do you think it would taste like? *(Let children offer their own ideas.)* Maybe it would taste like a marshmallow, or meringue, or pudding? What would the word *rock* taste like? Crunchy and gritty? Bitter?

Have you ever heard the expression "I'm gonna make you eat your words"? A person might say that if she heard someone say something that she wanted to prove wasn't true. Let's say that a kid was teasing another kid about her report card. One kid says, "You couldn't get an 'A' on your report card even if you went to school for a million years!" So the other kid says, "Just you wait! Next semester, I'm gonna make you eat your words!" And sure enough, next semester, after working really hard in school, the kid who was being teased shows up with straight A's on her report card. The other kid has to eat his words, take back what he said.

If we had to actually eat every word we spoke, do you think we'd be more careful about the things we said? Angry, mean words would not taste very good. Encouraging, kind

Saving the Ants

words, however, would probably be delicious! What sorts of words do you think would taste good? Any ideas? *(Let children offer their suggestions.)*

There is an interesting verse in the Bible where Jeremiah is talking to God and says, "[Your] words were found, and I ate them, and [your] words became to me a joy and the delight of my heart . . ." (Jer. 15:16 RSV). The words that God had spoken to Jeremiah must have been good, kind words, because Jeremiah thought they tasted delicious!

Think about the words you say today and how they might taste. If you find yourself saying something that you wouldn't want to taste, maybe you can think of something nicer to say that would taste much better.

To help you remember to use sweet words, I brought along some sweet letters today. Before you go back to your seats, I'd like everyone to take some letters from the bowl. I hope you have fun eating your words.

Thank you for your sweet words of love and encouragement, dear Lord. Put good words in our mouths today.

Notes

Junk Food

Preparation: Bring one candy bar along with a bowl of fruit to share. (Grapes make for tidy eating in church.)

Does anyone here ever eat junk food? What is junk food? Can you describe it or give some examples? *(Wait for answers.)* Yes, junk food is usually sweet or salty and crunchy, and we eat it just for fun. It doesn't really make a very healthy meal, does it? If we read the nutrition label on this candy bar, we can see how healthy it is for us. *(Read some of the information on the label.)* The candy bar doesn't do our body much good, even though it may taste good.

Do you think there might be any way that junk could get inside of us, other than eating it? When we look at something or listen to something, it goes into our brain, and we often remember it, don't we? Is there anything that we watch or listen to that might be of no value?

Think about that as I read again a verse from the psalm for today. Psalm 119, verse 37 says, "Turn my eyes from worthless things, and give me life through your word" (NLT). Another translation reads, "Keep me from paying attention to what is worthless; be good to me as you have promised" (TEV).

Do we sometimes pay attention to what is worthless? I can think of some television shows and movies I've watched that seemed to have no real value to them. They might have been fun to watch at the time, but after they were over, I thought, "That didn't teach me anything good; that was really a waste of time." They were like junk food for my brain.

Some of the "junk food," such as movies, television shows, or books that we take in, may not just be worthless, but harmful. If the things we watch have a lot of punching or swearing or people saying mean things in them, or if we watch movies or read books that are scary, it's like eating junk food that has gotten moldy. If I showed you some food that was old and moldy, would you eat it? No! None of us would put that into our mouth, would we? We need to be just as careful about what we put into our mind. If there's something yucky on television, what can we do? *(Let children give suggestions. Examples given might be, "Turn the television off," or "Leave the room," or "Suggest something better to do." Affirm the good suggestions.)*

I do have something with me this morning that's very healthy and worthwhile, and you can eat it. Before you go back to your seats, help yourself to some fruit! *(Pass around the fruit bowl.)*

Help us Lord, to turn away from the harmful, evil things of this world. Help us to seek the good and helpful things that turn our thoughts toward you.

Notes

Seventy Times Seven

Preparation: Bring a large pad of paper and a fat marker.

Have you ever hurt another person? If you've either accidentally or purposefully stepped on someone's foot, or pushed someone, or called your sister or brother a mean name, or made someone feel bad, raise your hand.

It happens to everyone, doesn't it? And if we do something wrong to someone else, what should you say to that person? How do you apologize? *(Let children respond.)* Right, you say, "I'm sorry." And hopefully, what does the other person say? *(Wait for an answer.)* Good. The person says, "I forgive you." Those are very important words. Let's all try saying "I forgive you." Ready? All together . . . "I forgive you."

Of course it feels bad when someone else hurts you, but how do you feel if you hurt someone else? That feels bad too, doesn't it? And when you say, "I'm sorry," and you really mean it, and the answer comes back, "You're forgiven," it's so good to hear those words!

How many times do you think we should forgive someone? *(Let children suggest numbers.)* Peter asked Jesus this very question. In Matthew, chapter 18, it says that Peter asked Jesus, "Lord, how often should I forgive someone who sins against me? Seven times?" "No!" Jesus replied to Peter, "Seventy times seven!" (vv. 21-22 NLT). How many times is that? Does anyone know? *(An older child may figure this out.)* 7 X 7 = 49, so 70 X 7 = 490! *(Write equation on the paper pad.)* That's a lot, isn't it?

If every one of you stepped on my toes and you said, "I'm sorry," and I said, "I forgive you," would I even come close to that number? No. This isn't an experiment that I want to try. But the point is that Jesus wanted to make sure that we keep on forgiving others. We need to forgive so many times that we lose count! It's something we need to be good at, so let's practice. When I say, "I'm sorry," you say "I forgive you." Okay, let's try it. *(Practice call and response. You can even encourage children to try saying "I'm sorry" to the congregation and have them respond accordingly.)*

You're all getting very good at this. Now the next time you need to use those words, it will be easier, because you've practiced so much.

Lord God, thank you for forgiving us so many times. Help us to be always forgiving to others.

Notes

Fair Wages

Preparation: Bring six fairly heavy books for volunteers to carry and four coins to pay volunteers.

Has anyone here ever worked to earn money? *(Wait for a response.)* What did you do? How long did you work? Were you tired when you got done? Those of you who have worked for money, did you think that the payment was fair?

Would anyone like to earn some money this morning? I need four volunteers. I'll give each of you a job and pay you when you're done. *(Choose four kids and have them line up.)* Now, I'll ask my first volunteer; if I pay you one nickel, will you carry these three books to the back of the church and up here to the front again, three times? *(If they agree, let them start right away, while you continue to speak.)* Now, to the second volunteer; will you carry two books down the aisle and back, two times? *(Let second volunteer begin their job.)* Now, the next; will you carry one book down the aisle and back just one time? *(They may begin.)* And for the last one; your job is to walk to the first pew and back. You don't have to carry any books.

Will all my workers come and receive their wages now? Here's a nickel for each of you, and I'm going to pay last the person that I hired first. *(Distribute the money.)* Everyone got the same amount, didn't they? Raise your hand if you think this is fair. Raise your hand if you think it's not fair, if you think the one who did more work should get more money.

Thank you, workers. You can sit down now and rest from your labors. Did you know that Jesus told a story much like

Saving the Ants

this? In Matthew, Jesus told his disciples that the kingdom of heaven is like a boss who went out early in the morning to look for workers to gather grapes in his vineyard. He told them what he would pay before they started, and he hired workers from early in the morning until late in the day. Some worked all day long and some worked for only one hour, but they all got exactly the same wage.

Jesus' disciples didn't think this was fair. They knew what the story meant. Jesus was talking about the kingdom of heaven. If you follow Jesus and obey him and love him, will you go to heaven when you die? Of course you will. What if someone asks Jesus into their heart just a few minutes before they die? They will go to heaven, too! It's sad that they had to spend most of their life without having Jesus as their friend, but even if someone doesn't know Jesus until the very end of their life, the Lord still welcomes them with open arms.

Thank you for the free gift of eternal life, dear Lord. Thank you for welcoming everyone with open arms, no matter where or when they accept your love.

Notes

Two-Faced

Preparation: Bring a couple of Halloween masks that aren't too scary.

I brought along a couple of extra faces this morning. *(Put masks on briefly.)* Here's one face, and here's another. Is this really my face? No, it's a mask, isn't it? I don't really have more than one face.

Have you ever heard of someone being "two-faced"? It doesn't mean that you actually have two faces, but it means that you sometimes act in two very different or opposite ways. For example, if Jane told Mary, "I really like you, Mary. You're my best friend," then later told Tom, "I don't like Mary. She's not my friend," you could say that Jane is two-faced.

The Gospel lesson today, from the book of Matthew, has a story about two sons. The father tells the first son, "Son, will you go and work in the vineyard today?" And the first son replies, "I will not." Later, however, he decides to obey his father and he goes and works. The father also asks the second son to work in the vineyard and the second son answers, "I go, sir" (vv. 28-30 NRSV). But this son does not go at all.

Now I'll ask you the same question that Jesus asked his disciples after they had heard this story; which son did what his father wanted him to do? *(Wait for answers.)* Yes, the first son did the right thing.

Were these sons two-faced? *(Wait for answers.)* Yes. Both of them said one thing and did the opposite. The first son said the wrong thing and did the right thing. The second son said the right thing and did the wrong thing.

Saving the Ants

In the end, do you think it's more important to say the right thing or to do the right thing? *(Let children respond.)* Actions speak louder than words. Of course, the best thing would be to both say and do the right thing.

After you go back to your seats, see if you can think of something you can do to show your family how much you love them. Then don't forget to really do it!

Help us to keep in mind the things that you want us to do, dear Lord, and give us the strength and courage to really do them.

Notes

The Gardener

Preparation: Bring flower stickers to hand out.

In the Old Testament reading this morning, the prophet Isaiah tells a story about someone who planted a garden. I want all of you to imagine that you are planting a garden. You want this garden to be very special and beautiful, so you begin by carefully preparing the soil. You take out all the rocks and dig up any weeds you find. You mix rich, black compost into the soil and rake the dirt so that it's soft and crumbly and ready to be planted. Then you start to plant your seeds. *(At this point, begin to put one flower sticker on each child, while you continue talking. You may, however, choose to hand out stickers at the end of children's sermon.)*

You choose only the best seeds to plant in your garden. The chosen seeds are planted with care. Every day the garden is watered, and watched. The birds that come to eat the seeds are chased away. The weeds that pop up in the garden are quickly pulled out and thrown away.

With a garden so well tended, do you think good, healthy plants will grow? *(Wait for responses.)* Your garden should produce beautiful, healthy plants, shouldn't it? What if you put all that work into your garden and the only thing it produced was weeds? No flowers, no fruit, only prickles and thorns. How do you think you would feel? *(Let children answer.)*

Do you know what happened to the gardener in the story Isaiah told? He planted grape vines and took good care of them, but his garden didn't produce good grapes.

God is like that gardener, and we're his plants. God takes good care of us and wants us to grow and do good things. When we turn away from God and do what we shouldn't, it's as if God's garden is wilting and filling up with weeds.

Do you think God feels sad when this happens? I'm sure he does. This morning, you all received flowers to help you remember that you are part of God's garden. Grow strong and bear good fruit!

Lord God, our Creator, thank you for making us and caring for us. Help us to grow like healthy plants and produce good things with our lives.

Notes

Rejoice Always

Preparation (Optional): Bring a few percussion instruments for the children to play during the song.

Rejoice! Rejoice! What does it mean to rejoice? Can anyone tell me when a good time to rejoice might be? (*Let children respond.*) We rejoice when we're happy, don't we? We rejoice when something good has happened.

How do we rejoice? Do we rejoice loudly or quietly? (*Wait for responses.*) We can rejoice in many different ways, can't we? Some people may like to jump up and down and make lots of noise to rejoice. You see that at soccer games or baseball games. If the team that you're rooting for wins the game, there's a lot of jumping up and down and yelling and cheering. You can rejoice quietly. At a wedding, people are very happy and rejoice when the couple gets married. You see people smiling and laughing and sometimes people are so happy, they even cry.

There are many different ways to rejoice, but when should we rejoice? Should we rejoice maybe once a month, or just once a week? Perhaps it would be good for us if we rejoiced every day. Do you know what the apostle Paul told one congregation? He said, "Rejoice in the Lord always; again I will say, rejoice" (Phil. 4:4 RSV). Rejoice always. Do you think that would be hard to do?

Could you rejoice if someone just called you a bad name or if you just lost your favorite toy? Would it be hard to rejoice if someone has just stepped on your toe? (*Children may respond.*) Sometimes it's hard to rejoice, but God wants us to rejoice always because we always have something to rejoice about. We rejoice because God loves us, and he always will.

I have a very simple song to teach you. It goes like this:

Rejoice in the Lord always, and again I say rejoice. *(Repeat this line.)*
Rejoice, rejoice, and again I say rejoice. *(Repeat this line.)* *(Can be sung as a round.)*

Now I'll hand out a few instruments, and we can all sing together. The congregation can join in, too, if they like.

We rejoice in your love, Lord. Make us always thankful for being your people.

Notes

Pay Your Respect

Preparation: Bring coins with heads on them. You could bring a penny to hand out to each child at the end of the sermon.

H as anyone ever asked you a trick question? *(Children may respond.)* Here's an example of what I mean by a trick question. What if you had two best friends, and someone asked you, "So, which one do you like best?" Well, you like both of them, but this person is asking you to choose only one. So this isn't really a fair question.

Jesus was asked a trick question by a group of Pharisees who wanted to get him into trouble. They asked, "Is it lawful to pay taxes to Caesar or not?" (Matt. 22:17 RSV). This was a trick question because if Jesus said that you should pay taxes to Caesar, most of the Jews there would be angry because they didn't like Caesar. But if Jesus said that you shouldn't pay taxes to Caesar, then the policemen might come and arrest him, because you had to pay taxes.

So Jesus took their trick question and turned it into a question about not just where you pay your money, but where you pay your respect. Jesus asked the Pharisees to show him the money that they pay taxes with, and they showed him a coin that was like this quarter. *(Show the quarter or other coin.)* Then Jesus asked them, "Whose picture and title are stamped on [this coin]?" "Caesar's," they replied. "Well then," [Jesus] said, "give to Caesar what belongs to him, But everything that belongs to God must be given to God" (Matt. 22:20-21 NLT).

This quarter has a picture of George Washington on the front of it; he was the first president of the United States. Well, we can't give this coin to George. He died a long time ago. But he represents the government, and we can pay our government the taxes that the country needs to provide us with roads, police officers, firefighters, parks, and so many other things.

We can give our money to the church to help support God's work. We can use our money to help support people that are telling people about Jesus. Although God does appreciate our offerings, he wants more than just our offering on Sunday morning. God wants us to pay him our respect, love, and obedience. God wants us to offer our whole selves to him and be willing to serve with all of our heart.

Lord, we offer to you our respect and our love and our obedience. We want to serve you with all of our heart.

Notes

The Greatest Commandment

Preparation (Optional): Bring heart-shaped stickers to distribute at the end of the message.

S ome of you probably know many of the commandments listed in the Bible. Can anyone tell me one of them? *(Let children respond.)* The Ten Commandments are:

1. You shouldn't worship anything or anyone other than God.
2. Respect God's name; it is special. Don't use it as a curse.
3. Remember the day of worship and keep it holy.
4. Respect your father and your mother.
5. Don't kill anyone.
6. Husbands and wives, keep your special love only for each other.
7. Don't steal from anyone.
8. Don't tell lies about your neighbor.
9. Don't be jealous of your neighbor's house.
10. Don't be jealous of your neighbor's family. Don't want for yourself anything that belongs to your neighbor. *(Paraphrase by author.)*

There are other commandments found in the Bible as well. Which one do you think is the greatest, most important commandment? *(Let children respond.)*

116   Saving the Ants

This is a question that the Pharisees used to test Jesus. The Pharisees were a group of people who went to church a lot, but they were not very loving. They asked, "Teacher, which is the most important commandment in the law?" Jesus replied, "'You must love the Lord your God with all your heart, all your soul, and all your mind.' This is the first and greatest commandment. A second is equally important: 'Love your neighbor as yourself.' All the other commandments are based on these two. . . ." (Matt. 22:36-40 NLT).

I want everyone to put up your ten fingers. Those stand for the Ten Commandments. Now turn your palms so that they're facing you and cross your hands on your chest. That is the symbol for love. All of the Ten Commandments are based on loving God and loving others. If we really do love God, we will naturally obey all Ten Commandments. The commandments are based on love and respect.

Thank you, God, for your set of rules based on loving you and others. Help us to keep all of your commandments out of love for you.

Notes

Be Prepared

Preparation: Bring two flashlights with spent or very dim batteries and extra batteries for only one of the flashlights.

In the Gospel lesson for today, Jesus told a story about ten maidens. Five were foolish and five were wise. The maidens were waiting for a bridegroom to arrive so that they could go to a marriage feast. But since most of you probably aren't real familiar yet with marriage feasts and bridegrooms, I will tell you a little different version of the story, and I'll need your help.

I need two volunteers to hold my flashlights. *(Hand out flashlights, one with extra batteries and one without extra batteries. Try to give the batteries to a child old enough to replace them without too much help.)*

One evening in the land of the Mighty King, there was a wonderful party planned. It would be held in the king's own castle. There would be feasting and music and dancing. At the end of the party, all the guests were welcome to stay at the castle as long as they liked. All came to the castle walls to wait for the king himself to arrive. He had promised to walk them through the secret passages and doors that led to the very center of the castle, where the feast would take place. Only the king knew the way.

The king told all of the guests that they might have to wait some time, but they had to be ready for him when he came. "Watch and wait," he said, "because you do not know that exact hour that I will come." Two young subjects of the king were waiting for him to arrive. They both had their trusty flashlights along and as it got darker, they both turned their lights on and waited for the king. They waited for a long time. The lights got dim and the two almost fell asleep. Suddenly, a shout rang out. "The king has arrived! Get up, turn on your lights and follow the king."

One of the subjects was foolish and had no extra batteries and couldn't follow in the dark. The other subject was wise and had brought along extra batteries. He quickly changed the batteries, got up, and followed the king into the feast. *(Help child change batteries.)*

The story is about what will happen at the end of the world when Jesus comes again. Nobody knows exactly when Jesus will return, but we know that Jesus will come to earth again. We need to always be ready, to be doing what God wants us to do. And with Jesus in your heart and God's love in your life, you will be ready for Jesus when he comes again.

Lord Jesus, thank you for your promise to return. Help us to be ready.

Notes

25th Sunday after Pentecost   Matt. 25:14-30

Use It or Lose It

J esus told many parables describing how we need to prepare for when he comes again. He really wanted his disciples to listen. Jesus' return is something to look forward
to, but it is also something for which we need to prepare.

Jesus told "The Parable of the Talents" as a way to show
how we should get ready for Jesus' return. I'll tell you a different version of that story.

One day, a school principal had to go on a long trip. She
called her three best students into her office. To the first student, she said, "God has blessed you with an ability to understand computers. I'm going to leave you with all these new
computers. I know you'll be able to make good use of them."

To the next student she said, "You have been blessed by
God with a sense of beauty and design. In the studio I have
left bolts of fabric, paint, and other art materials for you."

To the last student she said, "You have been blessed by
God with a listening heart and the ability to solve conflict and
to bring friends who are fighting together again. All that I have
to leave with you with are kind words and a smile."

When the principal returned to the school many months
later, she went to see what her best students had done with the
talents each were given. The first student showed her the
library where students could access other libraries and class-
rooms with cameras that looked in on scientific experiments
happening around the world. "Well done!" said the principal,
"More computers will be delivered tomorrow for you to use."

The second student showed her the assembly auditorium
that had been transformed into a fantastic stage with scenery

and curtains. The principal also saw that this student had painted large murals on the walls. "You have done a splendid job!" exclaimed the principal. "In the art room I have left brightly colored clay. Create any sculpture you like."

The principal looked for the third student. She crossed the playground where many students were arguing and found the third student crouched behind a tree, ignoring the arguing. She glanced over at her friends fighting, but didn't move from her spot. The principal was upset. "You could have used your gifts to bring harmony to the playground, but you did nothing," she said. "Your friends needed you and you did nothing to help them. I am very disappointed in you."

All of us have been given talents by God. If we do not share our talents, we disappoint God and our wonderful gifts are wasted. If we use our talents to help others, then we can be excited and happy to meet Jesus, knowing that we have done our best with what we have been given.

Thank you Lord, for giving us the ability to do so many wonderful things. We want to use our gifts to help others; help us to do this.

Notes

26th Sunday after Pentecost   Matt. 23:1-12

Showoffs

Preparation: Bring a phylactery and a prayer shawl, or pictures of each to help illustrate.

We know that God is love and that God sent Jesus into the world to save us because of his great love for us. But is God always happy with what we do? *(Let children answer.)* Jesus loves us, but sometimes the way we act can make him sad. We know that our parents love us, but if we do something wrong, we're going to get scolded, aren't we?

In Matthew, chapter 23, Jesus was talking to the crowds that had gathered around him, and he had some advice for them. He told the people to listen to the scribes and the Pharisees preach from the Bible, but he warned the people not to act like they do. Jesus said, "They crush you with impossible religious demands and never lift a finger to help ease the burden" (Matt. 23:4 NLT).

The burdens that the Pharisees were putting on the people were many little laws that the people were supposed to follow. For example, they expected the people to bring offerings of all kinds of food and spices. If someone used ten cups of flour to make bread one day, the Pharisees wanted them to bring one cup of flour as an offering to the temple. Most people were poor and worked hard all day long. They couldn't take the time to obey such laws. The Pharisees were rich and had time to obey their own laws.

Jesus scolded the Pharisees for making a big show of how they worshiped and how often they went to the temple. Many

Saving the Ants

Jews wore little boxes strapped to their forehead with a band of cloth; it was called a phylactery and it contained scriptures written on little pieces of paper. The Pharisees wore these also, but to make them more noticeable, they made them very large. The Pharisees also wore prayer shawls with very long fringes so that people would notice them and admire them.

The problem with all this was that the Pharisees didn't really care about impressing God. The Pharisees wanted to impress their neighbors instead. In other words, they were big showoffs. Do you think God is impressed by a showoff? *(Let children answer.)* God is pleased with the opposite of a showoff. To be the greatest in God's eyes is to be a humble servant. God wants us to serve him willingly just because we love him, not because we want other people to see the good things that we're doing.

Dear Jesus, may we always keep our eyes on you and not on ourselves. Help us to be your humble servants.

Notes

Overflowing Love

Preparation: Bring a small pot with a healthy flowering plant growing in it.

I brought a little plant with me this morning. It's a very nice-looking plant with green leaves and flowers. It has its own pot with lots of rich soil. How do you think I keep this plant healthy and growing? What do I need to do for my plant? *(Discuss with children; talk about water, sunshine, good soil, and so forth.)* I try to remember to give my plant the water and sunshine that it needs to grow.

Let's say I set my potted plant outside on a patch of bare dirt and then planted some seeds in the dirt around my pot, but only watered my plant and not the dirt around it. Would the seeds grow? *(Discuss with children.)*

What would happen if when I watered my own plant, I gave it so much water that lots of it spilled onto the dirt around it? Would those seeds in the dirt start to sprout? If they kept getting the extra water from the overflow, they would become healthy plants, too! My little plant wouldn't need all that extra water, and I'm sure that it wouldn't mind sharing.

One of Jesus' followers, Paul, traveled around the countryside encouraging new congregations that had just started after Jesus rose from the dead. He preached and wrote letters to them. In one of his letters to the Thessalonians, Paul wrote, "May the Lord make your love grow and overflow to each other and to everyone else, just as our love overflows toward you" (1 Thess. 3:12 NLT).

Why do you think Paul wanted their love to overflow? Wouldn't it be better if they had just enough love for themselves, like having just enough water for my one little plant? *(Talk it over with children.)* God doesn't want us to keep the love that he gives us to ourselves. He gives us so much love that it fills us up and overflows to others.

That love is like water; it brings life to people. And if someone has heard a little bit about Jesus and God's love, it's like a seed that has been planted in the dry soil. Then, when that seed is watered by love overflowing from God's people, like members of this congregation, the seed may sprout and that person may accept Jesus into their heart. Let's pray that all of us will let God's love overflow to others.

Thank you for watering our thirsty souls with your love, dear Lord. We pray that we let your wonderful love overflow to bless all those around us.

Notes

King and Shepherd

Preparation: Bring a large cardboard or wooden shepherd's staff to help "round up the sheep."

What does a king do? Can anyone tell me what the job of being king might be like? What sorts of things would you have to take care of? *(Let children respond.)* A king has to make laws. A king might have to be a judge and decide who is right. A king has to defend his country and his people from attacking armies. Do you think that a king has to take care of sheep? Does that sound like a job for a king? *(Children can answer.)*

Shepherding is a dirty, tiring job. You've got to chase after sheep all day, and then you have to sleep with them at night. If a wolf is running after your sheep, you have to run out and tackle the beast and protect your flock. Can you imagine a king in velvet robes and golden crown running around in a muddy pasture chasing sheep?

Well, today is Christ the King Sunday and we recognize that Jesus Christ is the Almighty King, ruler of heaven and earth. But the Old Testament reading describes the Lord God as a shepherd taking good care of his sheep. A king *and* a shepherd, those are the pictures we have of our Lord this Sunday.

Ezekiel 34 tells us what kind of shepherd our Lord is: "I myself will search for my sheep. . . . I will seek the lost, and I will bring back the strayed, and I will bind up the injured, and I will strengthen the weak" (Ez. 34:11, 16 NRSV). Even when the sheep are scattered all over the place, the shepherd will gather them up and bring them back. God always looks for us when we've turned away from him and have taken the wrong and dangerous path. Our Lord never gives us up for lost.

Would someone like to try shepherding this morning? *(Choose a volunteer and hand them the shepherd staff.)* Now, the rest of you are sheep. I'd like you to spread out here in the front. *(You may have to set boundaries so sheep don't get carried away.)* The shepherd needs to gather up his sheep and bring them back here to sit down again. The shepherd will walk around calling, "Here sheep! Come home!" And as soon as the shepherd touches you with his staff, you have to follow him. Make sure you touch everyone gently with your staff, shepherd. *(Help if needed.)*

Good job, shepherd. *(Sheep sit again.)* Jesus wants us to take care of each other just like he cares for us. He wants us to feed the hungry, take care of the sick, and even help people who have done bad deeds. By caring for others, we care for Jesus. Every one of you can be a good shepherd.

Jesus, you are our Good Shepherd. Thank you for your tender care.

Notes

Other Resources from Augsburg

Scolding the Snakes: and 58 Other Kids Sermons from the Gospel of Luke
by Ruth Gilmore
128 pages, ISBN 0-8066-4082-0

A volume of sermons for children designed for non-Lectionary churches and churches using Year C of the Revised Common Lectionary. Includes a CD-ROM that allows users to add personal touches to the sermons.

Barefoot in the Snow: and 51 Other Kids Sermons for Special Times and Topi
by Ruth Gilmore
128 pages, ISBN 0-8066-4083-9

A volume of sermons for children—52 in all—for each Sunday of the yea including holidays, special times, and topics. Includes a CD-ROM that allows users to add personal touches to the sermons.

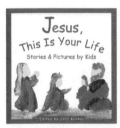

Jesus, This Is Your Life: Stories and Pictures by Kids
edited by Jeff Kunkel
48 pages, ISBN 0-8066-4165-7

A delightful collection of New Testament stories, retold and illustrated by kids. Readers of all ages will enjoy this collection.

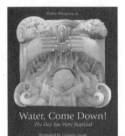

Water, Come Down! The Day You Were Baptized
by Walter Wangerin, Jr.
40 pages, ISBN 0-8066-3711-0

Beautifully told and illustrated, this is a wonderfully imagined story of God's power and love joined in the baptism event—a story that will grow richer in meaning each time the book is read

Available wherever books are sold.
To order these books directly, contact:
1-800-328-4648 • www.augsburgfortress.org
Augsburg Fortress, Publishers
P.O. Box 1209, Minneapolis, MN 55440-1209